Tribe Vibes

Building Friendships with Purpose and Heart

Heather Martin

Tribe Vibes

Copyright © 2024 Heather Martin
www.tribevibes.info
Book Design by Sandra Moreano
All rights reserved
ISBN: 978-1-7361250-5-2

All rights reserved.

No part of this publication may be reproduced, distributed, or transmitted in any form or by any means, including photocopying, recording, or other electronic or mechanical methods, without the prior written permission of the publisher, except in the case of brief quotations embodied in critical reviews and certain other noncommercial uses permitted by copyright law.

For my tribe
—past, present, and future—
who taught me the true meaning of friendship,
laughter, and showing up when it matters most.
This book is for you.

Table of Contents

Introduction: *The Journey to Fun, Fierce and Forever Friendships* 1
The Anatomy of Friendship: Why Your Tribe Matters 3
Tribe Check: Time to Reflect on Your Crew 5
Finding Your Tribe: Attracting the Right Vibes 7
Your Tribe Vibes: Friends in All the Right Places 11

THE FRIENDSHIP FOUNDATION: SETTING THE STAGE FOR STRONG BONDS

1. *Consistent Care: The Blueprint for Lasting Friendships* 17
2. *Give, Take, Repeat: The Art of Balanced Friendship* 21
3. *No More Excuses: Accountability in Action* 25
4. *True North: Letting Your Values Guide Your Friendships* 29
5. *When Time is Precious: Choosing Between Connection and Self-Reflection* 33
6. *Engage Fully: Let's Talk About Ditching Distractions!* 37

STRAIGHT TALK: NO FILTERS, JUST FRIENDSHIPS

7. *Communication: The Dance of Connection* 45
8. *Scooby Clues Not Needed: Let's Get Direct About Support* 49
9. *Timing is Everything: When to Give Your Friend the 411* 53
10. *Beyond Small Talk: The Power of Genuine Feedback* 59
11. *Disagreements Don't Have to Be a Disaster!* 65

THE FRIENDSHIP GLOW-UP: WHERE FEELINGS MEET GROWTH

12. *Growing Together: The Joy of Mutual Encouragement!* 73
13. *Dare to Be Real: The Power of Vulnerability and Authenticity* 79
14. *From Hurt to Healing: The Art of Apologies and Letting Go* 83
15. *Friendship Gratitude Goals: Reflect, Love, and Live with a Thankful Heart!* 89
16. *Friends Are Like a Puzzle: Each One Brings a Different Piece* 93

From Memes to Memories: The Fun Side of Friendship

17 Beyond the LOLs: Use Tech with a Flair! 99
18 Podcasts, Playlists, and Chill: Friendships at Play 103
19 Celebrate Like a Cheerleader: Pump Up Your Friends' Wins! 109
20 Create Shared Adventures: Turn Moments into Memories! 113

Through Thick and Thin: Friendship's Tough Stuff

21 Navigating Life's Storms: Being the Rock Your Friends Need 119
22 Lock It Down: Building Trust and Ditching the Drama 125
23 Friendship Fences: Respecting Boundaries with Love 129
24 Press Pause: When It's Time to Take a Break from a Friendship 135
25 When a Friendship Reaches Its Season: Knowing When It's Time to Let Go 139
26 Friends or Frenemies? Managing Jealousy and Hidden Tension 143
27 Letting Judgment Go: Respecting Friends' Viewpoints without the Side-Eye 147
28 Balancing Act: When Friends Don't Get Along 151

New Paths and Surprises: Embracing Change Together

29 Single, Married, & Still Surviving: Thriving through Life's Plot Twists 157
30 Swipe Right, Swipe Left: Being Your Friends Dating Wingwoman 163
31 Love in the Air: Don't Ghost Your Friends! 169
32 Bedroom Banter: How Much Do You Share? 173
33 Go with the Flow: The Art of Adaptability in Friendships 177
34 Rebuilding Bridges: How to Reconnect with Friends After Time Apart 181
35 The Roommate Remix: Friendship Meets Shared Spaces 185
36 Cubicle Chronicles: Juggling BFFs and Business in the Workplace 189

Together We Thrive

37 Emergency Contact Energy: Next-Level Friendship Care 197
38 The Power of the Collective: Uniting Your Tribe for Something Bigger 201
39 Spice It Up: Celebrating the Magic of Our Differences! 205
40 From Rivals to Rock Solid: Embracing Healthy Competition in Friendships 211

Conclusion 215
Acknowledgments 217
Appendix 219

INTRODUCTION
The Journey to Fun, Fierce, and Forever Friendships

When I think back to my childhood, I can still picture us racing down the street on our banana bikes, laughing as we drank from the garden hose without a care in the world. Friendships back then seemed easy to find and effortless to keep. But for me, moving frequently meant that finding my tribe was a lot of trial and error. Some faces remain vivid in my memories, while other names have long since faded. Yet, through all those years and changes, one thing has always been clear—we're all searching for that person who *gets us*, who wants to spend time with us and know us for who we are. Back then, finding time to make mixtapes, prank call friends, or set off on a spontaneous road trip without a Rand McNally roadmap was effortless. But as we grow older, free time shrinks, some seasons in life feel like a never-ending whirlwind, and no one's scheduling our playdates anymore.

Honestly, building *meaningful* friendships as an adult is like assembling IKEA furniture. It looks straightforward in the beginning, but halfway through you're wondering why you have extra screws, and what you thought was a chair is actually looking more like a bookshelf. Friendships aren't *supposed* to be confusing, but somehow they always find a way!

And don't even get me started on the group chats. One minute it's all LOL and memes, and the next, you're ghosted for *three days*. You start to wonder: "Do I even have a tribe anymore, or is it just me talking into the void?" Whether you're still rolling with your childhood crew or, like me, got thrown into the deep end of *Rebuild Your Social Life at 44*, friendships can get complicated. Spoiler alert—adulting and friendships aren't as easy as they made it look on *Friends*.

If I could find my tribe after a 25-year relationship hit the skids, a cross-country move, and a whole lot of awkward new-friend energy, then so can you. Building meaningful connections doesn't have to be stressful or cringey. With a little intention, a good dose of humor, and a willingness to dive into the fun of creating new connections, you'll find yourself surrounded by vibrant, fabulous friendships in no time.

Tribe Vibes grew out of necessity—I wanted to learn to be better at friendship. I wanted to practice friendship at a new level, and I needed a little handbook for myself to remind me how to be my authentic self, how to love on my friends, and how to build relationships with intention and care.

This book isn't a checklist you have to complete to be a "good friend." That's too much for anyone. Think of it as a guide you can come back to whenever you need a little nudge or some inspiration. You don't have to do everything all at once, or even anything at all. Sometimes, just one tip or gentle reminder is all it takes. If you try to digest everything in one sitting, it'll feel like you're overloading your plate at a buffet. So read it with a light heart. Let it be something you turn to when you're navigating specific situations or when you just want to check in with yourself about how you're showing up in your friendships.

As I put pen to paper, I came to realize that nothing in this book is earth-shattering or a grand revelation. It's a little bit of common sense, a dose of self-reflection, a drizzle of psychology, a pinch of introspection, and a whole lot of reminders. I've packed this book with easy advice and simple phrases you can use in real-life situations. Why? Because I know that even with the best intentions, we all need clear and actionable ways to put what we learn into practice. These practical actions and phrases will serve as touch-points, helping you approach your friendships with greater awareness and care. Whether it's figuring out how to set boundaries, offer support, or simply be a better listener, these tools are here to make that journey a little easier and more effective.

Let me tell you, I'm far from a perfect friend—I've made mistakes, stumbled, and learned a lot along the way. However, I'm committed to evolving as a person and nurturing relationships built on love, loyalty, and respect.

Are you ready? Good, because it's time to stop questioning where you stand with others and start deepening the connections that truly matter. Let's do this!

THE ANATOMY OF FRIENDSHIP
Why Your Tribe Matters

Friendships aren't just a *nice-to-have*—they're basically essential to living a happy, healthy life! From the good times to the tough stuff, having a solid group of people by your side makes everything better. In fact, science has your back on this one: Research shows that real human connections are like a secret hidden gem for your mental and emotional well-being. It's not just about having someone to text when you're bored; it's about cultivating those deep, laugh-till-you-snort, *I'll bring the tissues and the tequila* kind of support that make life way more colorful (and a lot more fun).

Strong friendships do more than just fill up your weekend plans. They boost your mood, lower stress, and help you regain your balance from life's unforeseen obstacles with a little more grace. Honestly, friendships are the best kind of therapy (and they don't bill you by the hour). At the heart of these connections? Trust and openness. When you can be your true, unfiltered self (sweatpants and all) around your friends, that's when the connection truly deepens. It's those late-night deep dives, the inside jokes, and the feeling that no matter what, someone has your back. That's what makes friendship so epic!

Sure, it's not all sunshine and selfies. Like anything worth having, friendships take a little work. Sometimes, things get messy, and you have to navigate the bumps in the road. But the payoff? Totally worth it. When you invest time and energy into building these bonds, you're not just creating good vibes for yourself—you're spreading positivity to the people around you. It's like throwing a rock in a pond; those ripples of kindness and connection go way beyond just your circle.

True friendships don't just make life sweeter—they inspire growth and self-discovery. Besties challenge your perspective, introduce you to new ideas, and give you that boost when you need it most. Strong connections can increase your resilience and even add a few extra years to your life (yeah, you read that right!). When you invest time and energy into your friendships, you're also investing in yourself.

So, next time you're laughing until your sides hurt, or having a deep heart-to-heart, remember—these moments aren't just fun, they are the bedrock of a happier, healthier life. Who knew that hanging out with your gal pals was basically the secret to immortality?

TRIBE CHECK
Time to Reflect on Your Crew

Before we get too far, let's take a little inventory of your current circle. Are your friendships lifting you up, or are some of them dragging you down like a laptop that keeps buffering during a crucial Zoom call? Be real with yourself: Are these the people who help you grow, push you to be better, and stay reliable, like a fully charged device on your busiest day? Or do some friendships feel like they're running on dial-up speed and sucking the life out of you? Your tribe should be like a power-up in a video game: giving you energy, pushing you forward, and making everything a bit more fun. You want friends who challenge you to aim higher, not ones who feel like that sticky gum you can't shake off your shoe. So, ask yourself: Are these relationships actually making you feel good, or are they obligations you dread?

Now let's look at the mix. Is your tribe as diverse as it could be? We're talking not just about backgrounds or experiences, but perspectives. Diversity in friendships brings new viewpoints, and who doesn't need a fresh outlook now and then? Having pals who challenge your thinking (without making you want to call a time out) can open up whole new worlds you didn't even know you needed in your life.

Speaking of give and take—are your friendships balanced? Like, really balanced? Are you giving as much as you're getting? It's worth asking yourself if your relationships feel reciprocal. In the best tribes, it's not all about what you can do for them or vice versa. There's a natural flow of support, empathy, and encouragement. It should feel like a two-way street, not a one-lane road to Burnout City.

And here's a big one: Are you spending time with people who share your passions? Do you have those friends who geek out about the same hobbies, career goals, or interests as you do? Shared interests are the magnetic pull that keeps a friendship connected, whether it's bonding over your love of hiking, reminiscing over '80s Saturday cartoons, or jamming out to live music. Those connections can bring you closer and make the time you spend together feel even more meaningful.

Finally, think about how often you actually connect. Are these relationships more than just quick likes on social media? Do you have meaningful conversations, or is everything stuck at surface level? Checking in on the depth and frequency of your interactions gives you a real sense of who's in your inner circle and who's actually on the outskirts.

Now, this isn't about categorizing your friends as good or bad like a reality show host deciding who gets the final rose. It's more about taking a step back and seeing which friendships are thriving and which might need a little extra TLC (or a hard reset). By doing this, you'll get a clearer picture of where you are at—and where you want to be—when it comes to your crew. Life's too short for weak signals and friendships that drain your battery.

FINDING YOUR TRIBE
Attracting the Right Vibes

We have established that life is better when shared with the right people—your tribe. You want those friends who stand by you, make you laugh until you cry, and know just what to say when life hits hard. But how do you actually find these magical humans?

Finding a friend can be a lot like dating, but somehow *weirder*. You're out there, trying to find *your people*, maybe accidentally oversharing about hours of scrolling through obscure Reddit threads or awkwardly asking, "Sooo, want to grab coffee sometime?" It's like being back in middle school, but with more responsibilities and less time to over analyze your outfits.

Know Yourself & What You Value
Before you find your tribe, it helps to know what you're looking for. What kind of friendships feed your soul? Do you crave deep, philosophical chats over coffee, or are you more into spontaneous adventures where anything could happen (yes, even karaoke at 2am)? Do you need a pep-talker, a partner-in-crime, or someone who keeps it real? Understanding your social style—whether you thrive in small, intimate gatherings or prefer a lively crowd—can help you find friends who match your vibe.

Think about your past friendships, too—what worked, and what didn't. Reflecting on those experiences can guide you toward connections that truly complement your personality and needs. And don't forget to consider where you are in life—whether you're focused on career growth, rediscovering old hobbies, or just looking for a fresh start, finding friends on a similar path can make the bond stronger. Knowing what you value helps you attract people who bring out the best in you, like curating a playlist that matches your personal rhythm.

Pursue Your Interests
Want to meet people who get you? Do the things you love. Whether it's joining a fitness class, a book club, or volunteering for a cause you care about, shared interests create easy and natural ways to connect with

others. Plus, you'll already have something to talk about that isn't the weather. Bonus—no socially clumsy small talk. It's like skipping the intro and going straight to the good part.

And heck, even if you're nervous, try something new. Stepping out of your comfort zone can lead to surprising connections. You never know who you'll meet at that painting class or trivia night—it could be your next adventure buddy or someone who shares your love of bad reality TV shows (yes, I am guilty here). Who knows? You might discover a new hobby while you're at it.

Be Open & Approachable
I don't know about you, but for me sometimes meeting new people can feel like I've been dropped into the middle of family-reunion talent show. Remember to smile (you've got a great one!), make eye contact, and genuinely ask questions. Showing real curiosity about someone else's experiences is the best way to build a connection, and they might be as nervous as you.

Strengthen Existing Connections
Sometimes your future tribe is hiding in plain sight. That coworker you always joke around with or that old friend you haven't seen since...well, who knows when? Maybe it's time to reach out and see if there's a deeper connection waiting to happen. Your tribe doesn't always have to be brand new. Even small, everyday interactions can turn into something meaningful.

For example, my medical assistant recently chatted with me during a routine visit, sharing a bit about her life, and before I knew it, she invited me to her Oktoberfest party. It was a simple moment that blossomed into a real connection, reminding me that sometimes all it takes is being open and paying attention to the people already around you. You never know when a casual conversation can lead to a new friendship or deepen an existing one.

Recognize Compatibility
Brace yourself. Not everyone you meet is going to be your person, and that's just how life is! Some relationships won't align with your values or your energy, and it's crucial to recognize when to step back or shift your focus. Think of it like tuning a radio—sometimes you hit the perfect

frequency, and everything clicks; other times, it's all static, no matter how much you adjust the dial. It's not about forcing a connection or fixing the static—it's about finding the stations that play the music you want to hear.

The key is knowing when to move on without feeling guilty or obligated to keep trying. It's okay to be selective about who you invest your time and energy in. Focus on the friendships that feel natural, mutual, and uplifting. After all, life's too short to waste time on connections that don't add value to your journey. Instead, save your energy for those who make life feel a little lighter and a lot more fun.

Create Opportunities for Connection
Sometimes you need to play the host. Organize a get-together, plan a fun activity, or invite a mix of friends to do something casual. Relationships grow in relaxed settings where no one's worried about impressing anyone, and who knows, someone might even introduce you to your next great friend!

Leverage Social Media (Yep, Really!)
Social media doesn't have to be just about inspirational quotes, cooking hacks and lurking your high school crush. Use it to find your people! Join groups that align with your interests, participate in community events, or connect with like-minded folks on LinkedIn, Instagram, or your local Facebook group. Your future best friend might just be a few likes and a direct message away.

Why Your Tribe Matters
Let's not forget that finding your tribe isn't just about fun and games—you are making a choice to surround yourself with people who make you better. These are the folks who'll help you shine, share in your triumphs, and hand you tissues during your low moments (or wine—depends on the friend). And trust me, those people? They're priceless.

As you put yourself out there, remember: Finding your tribe isn't a race. Take the time to build real, meaningful relationships, one moment, one shared laugh, and one heartfelt conversation at a time.

YOUR TRIBE VIBES
Friends in All the Right Places

Not all friendships are created equal, some are deep enough to handle your midday crisis texts, while others are lighter, more casual connections. Knowing where each friend stands helps you appreciate the unique value they bring to your life and ensures you invest the right energy in the right places. By identifying your tribe, you can better understand which relationships nurture you and provide the support you need for personal and professional growth. After all, not every friendship will reach the depth of an inner circle, and that's how it should be.

Here's how you can break down your tribe:

Inner Circle
Your inner circle consists of those ride-or-die friends who truly know you inside and out. These are the ones who've stood by you through *everything*, sharing in your triumphs and standing by you in every season. They provide a safe space for vulnerability, where you can express your fears, share your dreams, and seek advice without judgment.

This group is often a delightful mix of childhood pals, college buddies, neighbors and the mom friends you've met at school events or playdates. They may not all know each other, but that doesn't matter—they are YOUR people. They understand your quirks, laugh at your inside jokes, and will always remind you of the time you tripped at that party or wore two different shoes to work.

These friendships feel like home, a sanctuary where you can let your guard down and just be yourself. And yes, they probably have a treasure trove of embarrassing photos that you hope never resurface, but that's just part of the love and laughter you share.

Close Friends
Important in your life and often around for the big moments, these friends are close, but maybe you're not calling them after that weird date to dissect every detail. You see or talk to them regularly and share meaningful conversations, but there might be a bit of a boundary when it comes to your innermost thoughts and feelings. Think of them as your

"inner circle lite"—still incredibly special, with maybe fewer pajama parties.

Casual Friends
These friends are fun to be around. You probably wouldn't call these friends if you were having an existential crisis, but they're the best company for a concert in the park or a spontaneous adventure. While you don't necessarily dive into life's deepest topics with them, they still bring joy and variety to your life. Not every friendship needs to be deep—sometimes, a good laugh over brunch is just as valuable.

Acquaintances
These are the people you see in passing—at work, the gym, or through mutual friends. You share friendly conversations, but the relationship doesn't extend much beyond small talk. They're like the background music of your social life—pleasant, but not the main event. Recognizing these connections for what they are can help you focus your emotional energy on more meaningful relationships.

Professional Friends
These friendships bridge the gap between colleagues and confidantes. You bond over career wins, swap LinkedIn tips, and collaborate on projects, but the relationship typically stays work–focused. Professional friends play an important role, helping you grow and develop at work. The twist is that sometimes, with the right vibe and shared experiences, these work buddies become more than just professional connections. Just because a friendship starts with spreadsheets doesn't mean it won't one day include sharing photos of your cat in a birthday sweater.

Activity–Based Friends
These friends come into your life through shared hobbies or sports. You bond over common interests, and your interactions often center around that activity. While the connection might not go deep outside of your shared interest, these friendships can still be incredibly fulfilling and provide a sense of belonging in those areas of your life.

Long–Distance Friends
Who says distance weakens friendships? Long–distance friends can absolutely be part of your inner circle, even if they're thousands of miles

away. These are the friends who've survived time zones, missed calls, and marathon text convos where you both randomly disappear mid-conversation. You may not talk every day, but when you do, it's like no time has passed at all. Whether you're sending voice notes about life's highs and lows or planning visits months in advance, these friendships are built on deep connection and mutual effort. In fact, the distance only makes your bond stronger—because when a long-distance friend is part of your inner circle, they're not just there for the big stuff, they're right there in spirit for the small moments too.

Childhood Friends

These friends have seen you through your awkward phases (and possibly own Polaroids as proof), and you share a history that goes way back. Even if you don't see them often, these friendships are like a vintage bottle of wine—aged to perfection. While you may have grown in different directions, the bond you share remains remarkable.

Why Identifying Your Tribe Matters

When you dive into this book, you'll move beyond casual friendships to focus on identifying and fortifying your inner circle—the people who truly matter in your life. It's a journey toward getting crystal clear on who will be there to celebrate your victories, sit with you through your struggles, and help you grow. The goal is to strengthen those deep, meaningful connections that shape your life, your self-worth, and your future.

This book is your guide to not just finding your tribe but cultivating a circle of people who reflect your values, uplift your spirit, and challenge you to be your best. These are the friendships that aren't just for the fun moments—they're the foundation of your personal growth and fulfillment. As you read, you'll learn to invest in the relationships that matter most, strengthen the bonds that truly define you, and ultimately create a tribe that empowers you to thrive.

The Friendship Foundation
Setting the Stage for Strong Bonds

There are endless books on how to nurture romantic relationships, but when it comes to friendships—the bonds that carry us through life's highs and lows—where's the guidebook to help them truly thrive? Cultivating strong friendships takes intention, something I craved but didn't always know how to create. I wanted deeper connections but often found myself without the right tools. So, while this book may at first feel like a to-do list, it's truly a reflection of the many seasons I've navigated in life—each one bringing clarity to what I wanted, what I wouldn't settle for, and choosing to invest in the ones that align with who I am and who I'm becoming.

Now, at 50, I've come to understand that some relationships are for a season, others for a reason, and a rare few are for a lifetime. I want to deepen my self-awareness, invest in friendships that will grow with me and create bonds that will truly endure.

There was a time when I poured everything into my friendships, giving my time, my energy, and my heart, only to feel completely drained afterward. I'd hop on the phone, listen, support, and offer advice, but somewhere along the way, I forgot that friendship is a mutual exchange. I was showing up for others but forgetting to make space for myself. Then it hit me—the most important friendship I could nurture was the one with myself.

Building that relationship with myself became a foundation for all my other friendships. I started to check in with myself. What do *I* need today? What fills *my* cup? In learning to support my own well-being, I found I could show up more fully for others without feeling drained. Self-friendship taught me to listen to my needs, to set healthy boundaries, and to prioritize my own joy and peace. It's a reminder that the stronger my relationship with myself, the more vibrant and balanced my connections with others become.

What I have learned through these collective moments is that friendships need care and attention to thrive, but without pressure or guilt. It's okay to forget a call or miss a coffee date because true friendships don't have to feel like a chore. What they do need is intentionality—a gentle effort to stay connected, even in the midst of busy lives. And part of that effort comes from knowing and living by your values. Values are like the North Star—without them, we risk drifting aimlessly in our friendships. If I claim to value health but my Peloton is gathering dust, am I truly living by what I say matters most? When we're clear about our values and live them out, we draw in the people who truly get us, who see and respect us for who we really are. It's those small, thoughtful actions and shared values that help friendships grow strong and deep, showing your friends, "I'm here, and I've got you."

As you dive into each section, you'll find a mix of metaphors, stories and some actionable steps. There's a lot of detail here because friendships, just like life, are nuanced and layered. But don't feel like you need to absorb it all at once. Take small bites, reflect, and maybe even journal along the way. This book, like friendships, is meant to be enjoyed over time, not rushed. It's designed to give you the tools to identify those meaningful relationships that make up your inner circle, the friendships that last a lifetime. Take your time, enjoy the process, and remember—building strong, lasting connections can be as rewarding as it is fun.

1

CONSISTENT CARE
The Blueprint for Lasting Friendships

Friendships are like building a house—it's not the flashy furniture or fancy paint job that makes it last. Nope, it's all about the foundation, the structure, and the steady bricks you lay over time. Trust isn't built on grand gestures; it's created through consistency. Each time you show up for your friends, respond to a message, or follow through on a plan, you're laying another brick in the wall of trust. Over time, these small, dependable actions become the backbone of a rock-solid foundation.

What makes friendships feel secure is the steady presence that friends provide. It's like the comfort of your favorite coffee shop, always getting your order just right. In friendships, it's those little things—like recalling their go-to comfort food, showing up when you promised, or reaching out when they had a tough day—that create a sense of reliability. Each action adds another layer, reinforcing the feeling that you're not just passing through their life—you're a cornerstone, a constant they can count on.

Now, let's be clear—you're not expected to build a mansion overnight. Friendship isn't about being available 24/7 like an emergency repair service. Instead, it's about those small, thoughtful moments that remind your friends, "I'm here for you." Whether it's spontaneously bringing over a cozy blanket when they're feeling down or leaving a handwritten note just because, each of these moments adds a new layer of strength to the relationship. Eventually, this steady effort turns into something strong and lasting, a friendship that feels like home.

Think of it like maintaining a well-loved home. It's not the one big renovation that makes a house feel solid; it's the regular upkeep, the small, consistent efforts that add warmth and stability. Friendship is the same way. Your ongoing efforts build a sense of comfort and security, like a heartfelt home where both of you know you belong. Each small act, like patching up a wall or tightening a loose handle, keeps the foundation strong. You're not just adding decoration—you're reinforcing the walls that make the friendship feel like a place you can always come back to.

In any well-built structure, it's the steady work that holds everything together, but it's the personalized touches that make it truly feel like home. You are not on autopilot—you are adding those unique details that make a friendship special. Maybe you're the friend who remembers their go-to coffee order or the one who sends an encouraging text when it's needed most. These little moments, like hanging a funky piece of art, add character and warmth to the relationship. They aren't just bricks—they're the finishing touches that make the space feel uniquely yours.

Sure, life happens. Sometimes weeks go by without a word, and suddenly that house of friendship feels a little neglected. But just like maintaining that well-loved home, a little regular upkeep can make all the difference. Think of it as clearing the leaves from the gutters or giving the walls a fresh coat of paint—small efforts that keep everything in good shape. Schedule those coffee dates, FaceTime chats, or quick *thinking of you* texts. You don't need a major renovation—just consistent care and attention to keep the friendship from falling into disrepair.

My Personal Cheat Sheet for Life's Moments

For me, I can't rely solely on memory to keep track of all the important dates, so I've turned to my iPhone Reminder app. It's my personal assistant in my pocket, filled with birthdays, anniversaries, and quirky events like my friend's cat's birthday. I've set reminders weeks in advance when a gift is needed, because life gets busy, and it's easy to forget those little things. The part I love is when that notification pops up, and I send a quick "Happy Birthday to Fluffy," which often leads to a fun, lighthearted moment that strengthens my bond with my friends. It's not just about remembering the date—it's about showing up consistently, time after time, so they know they matter. Each reminder is a chance to say, "I see you, I'm thinking of you, and I'm here," even in the small moments.

These consistent acts create a sense of stability and trust, letting them know you're someone they can rely on. Over time, it becomes clear that you'll always be there—not just for the big events but for the little, everyday moments too—showing that their friendship truly means something to you.

Blueprint for Friendship Success

- **Create a Building Schedule:** No, you don't need actual blueprints, but setting reminders for regular check ins works wonders. It's like a construction timetable for your friendship. Is a big day coming up for your friend? Drop them a quick text to say, "You've got this!" If you've got a group of friends, why not create a shared calendar for birthdays, milestones, or random hangouts? These small, scheduled moments keep your friendship house from feeling neglected.

- **Fix the Cracks Before They Spread:** Noticed your friend's been quieter than usual or hasn't reached out in a while? Send a quick check in, like "Hey, thinking of you!" It's like fixing a small crack before it becomes a bigger problem. By staying consistently connected you keep your friendship house from falling into disrepair.

- **Build with Personalized Care:** Consistency doesn't mean doing the same thing over and over; it's about showing up regularly in ways that make a friend feel valued. Personalize how you connect to keep things fresh—a quick text one day, a thoughtful check in the next, or a surprise BBQ when you both need some fun. Like adding unique decor to a home, these thoughtful gestures make your friendship feel warm, secure, and one-of-a-kind.

- **Communicate Your Construction Timeline:** If you're in a busy season or need a little downtime, that's okay—just let your friends know. It's like letting your contractor know when the next phase of work can start. By sharing when you'll be available to hang out or catch up, you maintain trust and ensure that no one feels left out or unappreciated. Transparency helps keep the friendship on track, even when life gets hectic.

At the heart of every strong friendship is a sturdy, well-built foundation. You don't need massive, show-stopping moments to keep the house standing—just regular, consistent, dependable actions that tell your friends, "I'm here." Whether it's an ugly cry on a bad day, a celebration of their latest win, or just sitting in sweats binge-watching TV, these small moments are the bricks that build trust. Grab your hard hat, lay those bricks, and build that friendship house strong enough to last a lifetime.

2

GIVE, TAKE, REPEAT
The Art of Balanced Friendship

Now that we've laid the foundation, let's talk about what keeps that friendship house standing strong—reciprocity. It's an extraordinary balance where everyone feels valued and supported. You have those good vibes bouncing back and forth like a never-ending game of friendship ping-pong. Remember this is not about keeping score. It is authentically and genuinely showing up for each other with love and intention.

In that well-played game of ping-pong, both friends take turns sending the ball back and forth, keeping the momentum going. Friendships are much the same—each person contributes in their own way, whether it's offering a listening ear, giving thoughtful advice, or bringing some much-needed laughter. Some days, you're the one returning the serve, offering support when they need it most. Other days, they're the ones ready to volley back when you're feeling down. It's this rhythm—each person taking their turn—that keeps the friendship balanced and ensures that both sides feel valued.

Matching energy is understanding what your friends need and bringing a vibe that complements theirs. If your friend is having a rough day, maybe it's about being a calm presence and offering a listening ear without trying to fix everything. On the flip side, when they're feeling celebratory, you match that excitement, becoming their biggest cheerleader. It's being in tune with where they are emotionally and responding in a way that feels like a natural extension of the connection you share.

It's like a seesaw, where sometimes you're the one lifting them up, and other times, they're bringing you back into balance. Maybe one week, you're the friend who picks up the phone to check in, asks about their work project, and listens as they vent about a tough situation. You're there with an open ear and a "Let's get through this together" attitude, helping them carry the weight of whatever is on their mind. Then, a few weeks later, they're the ones reaching out to you when you've gone quiet, reminding you that you're not alone. They say, "I've got you—let's talk it out," and suddenly, that load you were carrying feels a little lighter.

And just like a seesaw, the most rewarding moments are when both friends are in sync, moving through life's ups and downs together—when they're the one who pulls you out of your comfort zone and drags you to a new dance class, and then later, you're the one inviting them over for a quiet night in when they need a break from the chaos. It's those little shifts—those moments when roles change and evolve—that make the friendship dynamic and alive.

The give-and-take is about having a rhythm where no one is stuck in just one role. It's about recognizing when to step up and when to step back, knowing that each friend has something different to offer at different times. Sometimes you're the rock, and sometimes you need a rock to lean on. This balance ensures that neither friend feels like they're always giving or always taking, but instead, that they're in a partnership where both sides feel supported and valued.

Linda's Thoughtful Teas & Reciprocity in Action
I have this *rockstar* friend, Linda, who is the absolute queen of kindness. When I was down and out with COVID, she dropped off this killer medicinal tea, throat lozenges, and a magazine right at my door. Linda's generosity doesn't stop there; she's constantly doing sweet, thoughtful things for everyone in her circle. Now, it's not about me matching her energy with the exact same gestures, but it's about showing up for her in a way that says, "I see you, I appreciate you, and I'm here for you, too." When her birthday came around, I made sure she had a beautiful bouquet of flowers waiting. When she was struggling with her job, I said, "Let's work on your LinkedIn profile together."

Reciprocity isn't a tit-for-tat game; it's a rhythm of showing love and attention in ways that matter to your friends. It's giving and receiving with open hearts, knowing that what you pour into the friendship will come back in beautiful, unique ways.

Reciprocity Rules: How to Keep the Balance in Friendship
- **Give & Receive with Intention:** Instead of just offering vague help, be specific about how you can show up for each other. For example, if your friend is feeling overwhelmed, say, "I've got some free time this Saturday—how about I help with [insert task]?" On the flip side, don't be afraid to ask for something specific in return, like, "Could you check in with me next week? I've got a tough meeting, and I'd love your encouragement afterward."

- **Read Each Other's Energy:** Pay attention to what your friend needs in the moment. Are they looking for a problem-solver, a cheerleader, or just a quiet presence? And when you're struggling, say what kind of support you need, too. Let them know if you need advice or if you're just looking for someone to listen. This mutual awareness keeps the rhythm of support flowing smoothly.

- **Allow Roles to Shift:** Recognize that roles in a friendship aren't fixed. One week, you might be the motivator, and the next, you could be the one needing reassurance. Embrace these shifts, knowing that it's okay to be the one needing support sometimes. Reciprocity means letting go of the pressure to always have it together and allowing yourself to lean on each other when needed.

- **Address Imbalances with Care:** If you notice that the give-and-take isn't feeling balanced, have an honest conversation about it. For example, you might say, "I've noticed I've been leaning on you a lot lately—let me know if there's anything you need from me." This creates space for open dialogue, ensuring that both friends feel valued and heard without keeping score.

Want to keep that good energy flowing? Next time you hang out, think, "How can I brighten their day, just a little?" And remember, this isn't a one-sided game—it's a give-and-take, where you both share the load and the laughter. Let your friends be there for you too, offering their support when you need it. The best friendships create a cycle of positivity, where each person gets their turn to lift and be lifted. After all, who wouldn't want to be part of a friendship that feels like a never-ending dance, where the steps might change, but the music keeps playing.

3

NO MORE EXCUSES
Accountability in Action

We've explored how consistency builds a strong foundation and how reciprocity creates a balanced give-and-take, but there's another key ingredient that holds everything together—accountability. It's what keeps us honest and makes sure we show up as the friend we aspire to be, even when things get tough. Okay, okay, I know—*accountability* sounds like something you'd hear in a corporate meeting, right? Trust me, in friendships, it's a total game-changer. Think of it less like a corporate buzzword and more like project management software that keeps everything running smoothly. Without it, things get glitchy fast! This is all about keeping the good vibes vibing and actually showing up when you say you will. When you establish accountability, your friendships go from casual hangouts to "We've got each other's backs for life" status.

In your inner circle, fostering accountability is like setting the tone for how you roll together. You know, being that friend who keeps it real, sticks to what they say, and isn't afraid to own it when things go off-track. It's not about calling anyone out—it's creating a space where everyone feels comfortable being upfront and honest. If someone slips up or crosses a boundary (or accidentally binge-watches the entire season without you—oops), it's handled with a mix of care and straight-up communication. That's what strengthens the bond!

When accountability is part of the friendship DNA, it's a team mentality—everyone's got skin in the game. No one is perfect, and that's okay. It's about owning up to your mistakes, saying, "Hey, I dropped the ball on this," or gently pointing out when your friend isn't being true to the values you both hold dear. It's the willingness to have the uncomfortable conversations, to be vulnerable and say, "I messed up," and to also hear, "You could have done better." *Those* are the conversations that build a friendship that's not just surface-level but built to last.

Keeping Friendships Real & On Point!
After my divorce, I thrust myself into the dating world for the first time in over 25 years. The dating scene had changed drastically from what I remembered—swipe this way, swipe that way, FaceTime meet-and-

greets, dating apps that felt more like social experiments, and, of course, the occasional date gone hilariously wrong. I was excited and nervous all at once. My friend Charlotte was there by my side through the whole transition, offering support and sharing in both my dating wins and my flops. We spent countless hours chatting and laughing together about this new world I was exploring.

But as I started to prioritize dates over my friendship with her, I didn't realize the impact it was having on her. Sure, I'd make plans with her, but if a date popped up, I was quick to reschedule or cancel altogether. I wasn't thinking about how it made her feel—I was just caught up in the whirlwind of this new chapter in my life.

One afternoon, Charlotte came to me in the most loving and honest way. She sat me down and said, "I realize you're enjoying getting back out there, but I have to be honest—it's starting to feel like I'm not as important anymore. I miss our time together." At that moment, it hit me. I hadn't realized just how much I had been neglecting our friendship. I was swept up in the excitement of dating, and Charlotte had been feeling sidelined.

She wasn't angry or accusatory; she was simply holding me accountable to the friendship we had built over the years. I realized that while I had been there for her in the past, I wasn't being present in the way she needed me to be now. She had every right to call me out—she cared enough about our friendship to speak up, and I knew I needed to listen.

At first, her words stung, not because she was harsh, because she was right. I had taken our friendship for granted in the midst of this new adventure. But her honesty was the push I needed to realize how I was showing up for the people who mattered most. I didn't want our friendship to feel like an afterthought, so I had to step up.

I made changes. I held myself accountable, by spending more time with Charlotte, and being more intentional about it. We made plans and stuck to them, and I made sure to check in with her as much as I was checking my dating apps. Our friendship strengthened because she wasn't afraid to call me out when I needed it.

Charlotte's approach also taught me something about holding friends accountable. It wasn't about blame or judgment—it was about reminding me of the value of our friendship and ensuring it stayed strong. Sometimes, accountability means having uncomfortable conversations, and that's okay. We can all lose sight of things sometimes, and true friends help each other stay on track.

Friendship isn't always easy—it requires effort, communication, and yes, I will say it again, accountability. Just as I needed Charlotte to hold me accountable, there have been times I've had to do the same for her. It's not a tally of who does what, but about being there for each other, even when things feel a little off. And when accountability is at the heart of a friendship, you know you've got something real and lasting. That's what makes it so valuable—it's a mutual commitment to show up, not just when it's convenient, but when it matters most.

Accountability Essentials

- **Hold Each Other to Promises:** Accountability doesn't mean nagging. If your friend promised to help with something or to be there for a big event, don't hesitate to give a little nudge: "Hey, are we still on for this?" It keeps things light and avoids the classic last-minute flake. It's not about perfection; it's about following through.

- **Own Your Mistakes:** When you mess up, be quick to admit it. Something like, "Hey, I know I didn't follow through on our plans last week, and I'm really sorry about that" shows maturity and responsibility. Owning up to your mistakes builds trust and makes it easier for your friends to feel comfortable doing the same. It creates a space where honesty is the norm.

- **Give Props for Stepping Up:** When one of your friends handles a tough convo like a pro or just nails that accountability moment, say something! "I see how you handled that, and it was awesome." A little recognition goes a long way in reinforcing that trust and showing that you value honesty.

- **Turn Accountability into Growth:** Approach accountability as a way to grow individually and together. When someone points out something you could work on, take it as an opportunity to improve. Say something like, "Thanks for telling me—I'll do better next time." This keeps the friendship positive and forward-thinking, turning tough moments into chances to strengthen your bond.

Accountability isn't about being the friendship police or tallying efforts—it's more about keeping it real and fair. It's creating a friendship culture where being transparent and responsible is the norm. When everyone's on board with that, your circle is not just tight—it's solid!

4

TRUE NORTH
Letting Your Values Guide Your Friendships

Friendships aren't just about finding people who love the same TV shows or share your obsession with hiking—they are also about connecting with people who understand and respect your values. If you are looking for deeper, more meaningful friendships, knowing what you stand for is key. If you don't know what's important to you, how can you expect others to? Getting clear on your values is like creating your personal user manual, and it's essential for building meaningful, lasting friendships.

Knowing Your Values Is Key

Think of your values as your personal GPS—they guide your choices, how you live your life, and who you spend time with. When you know what you stand for, you walk through life with a little extra swagger. It's like having a neon sign over your head that says, "I know who I am, and I'm sticking to it!"

Picture this: You've got a friend who lives for the party scene, but your ideal evening involves early mornings and health routines. You're not judging their choices (well, maybe just a little), but after one too many nights out, you start feeling out of sync. Recognizing your own values—health, balance, maybe a touch of tranquility—helps you see why this situation isn't quite aligning. Staying true to your values doesn't mean losing friends; it means finding friendships that support your well-being.

Sharing Your Values with Others

Once you've got your values locked in, the next step is sharing them with the people around you. It might feel a little tricky at first, like trying to explain to your grandma what TikTok is, but it's all about communicating what makes you feel comfortable and respected. It's important to understand that sharing your values isn't about forcing your beliefs on anyone—it's a way to express what makes you feel comfortable and respected.

For example, if your friend likes to plan last-minute weekend getaways, and you value keeping weekends free for family time, you could say, "I love that you're always up for an adventure, but weekends are when I try to focus on time with my family. How about we plan a day trip during the week instead?" It's all about communicating your needs without making them feel judged. You're just letting them know what aligns with your values—and a real friend will appreciate that honesty.

Values Attract the Right Friends
Values have a way of attracting the right people. When you live in a way that reflects what truly matters to you, you create space for friends who understand and respect you. It's easier to say 'no' to things that don't fit and 'yes' to what truly feels right. Friends who respect your values are the ones cheering you on, not making you feel like the odd one out for choosing family game night over a girls' night at the club.

At the same time, remember that your friends have values, too, and they might be different from yours. Balancing these differences and finding the sweet spot where you both feel respected is part of the journey. It's this understanding that allows you to grow individually while strengthening your friendships.

Financial Honesty
My girlfriend Mary, a single mom of three, loved spending time with her close-knit circle of friends, but there was one issue that kept coming up—their love for lavish outings. From fancy dinners to expensive weekend trips, Mary often found herself feeling the financial strain as she tried to keep up with their luxurious lifestyle. Her values were rooted in financial responsibility, especially as she was focused on making ends meet for her kids.

After attending one too many pricey gatherings, Mary knew it was time to speak up. She sat down with her friends and explained her situation, expressing how much she valued their time together but needed to prioritize financial balance. She wasn't asking them to stop enjoying the things they loved, but she needed to find ways to maintain her budget without feeling pressured to participate in expensive activities.

To Mary's surprise, her friends were incredibly understanding. They brainstormed new, budget-friendly ways to hang out—movie nights, potluck dinners, and even DIY spa days. The relief Mary felt was immediate. By sharing her values around financial balance and responsibility, she not only maintained her friendships but also deepened them. Her friend's willingness to adapt showed that true friends respect each other's needs, even when they come from different financial realities. This experience reinforced Mary's belief that sticking to her values wasn't about limiting her life—it was about making space for connections that genuinely supported her well-being and that of her family.

Tips for Living Your Values Out Loud

- **Define Your Values & Use Them as a Guide:** Identify your top 3-to-5 core values—whether it's health, loyalty, or self-improvement—and use them as a guide in your friendships. If something feels off, ask, "Does this align with my values?" If not, it's time to adjust—like switching from regular coffee to decaf when the jitters hit.

- **Express Your Values & Offer Options:** When talking about what's important to you, use 'I' statements to keep it honest without sounding judgmental. For example, you could say, "I'm more into relaxed, low-key activities these days." Instead of a flat out "No," try offering a suggestion that fits your values: "How about we do a picnic instead of going out late?"

- **Finding Common Ground:** Don't assume your friends *share* the same values. Ask them what's important and find ways to meet in the middle. For example, if your friend loves late nights and you prefer mornings, "I'd love to meet for a coffee date instead—mornings are more my speed."

- **Consistency Speaks Volumes:** Show your values through consistent actions, like prioritizing wellness with a regular morning walk or quiet time for self-care. Consistently living your values reflects who you are draws in friends who support and understand those choices.

Living out your values is key—talking about them is one thing but embodying them in your actions is where it truly resonates. When your friends see you prioritizing your well-being, they're more likely to respect that part of you. Whether you're inviting friends to join you at a yoga class or showing them how you balance work with self-care, leading by example draws in those who value similar things. And remember, these small actions over time will naturally shape your friendships in a way that feels authentic and fulfilling. Plus, sticking to your values helps you attract the right people into your life—the ones who really get you.

5

WHEN TIME IS PRECIOUS
Choosing Between Connection and Self-Reflection

Even in the strongest, most accountable friendships, there's one more thing to keep 'in check'—balance. I believe friendships are a bit like phone batteries. When they are fully charged, things are smooth, you are constantly connected, and everything is running at 100%. But if you're not careful, you can end up at 1% with the low-battery warning blinking in your face. As with your phone, you need to recharge *before* you hit zero.

However, it's not just about finding balance in your friendships; it's also about nurturing the most important relationship you have—the one with yourself. You can't pour from an empty cup, and if you're constantly giving to others without taking time to recharge your own internal battery, you risk becoming a friend who's only there in body, not in spirit.

It's tempting to say *yes* to every invite, every call, every random "Let's hang out!" because, hey, you want to be the friend who's always there! But if you're constantly in social mode, you'll start running on empty, and trust me, no one's at their best when their energy levels are in the red. Think of it this way: You can't scroll Instagram on a dead phone, and you can't show up for your friends when your own personal battery's drained.

So, give yourself permission to turn off the notifications, cancel the social plans, and dedicate time to recharge your internal battery—whether it's a solo puzzle session, journaling, or just staring at the ceiling in peace. Embrace the idea of being your own best friend, as it sets the stage for stronger, healthier relationships with those around you. Don't worry, your friends will still be there when you've powered back up.

The Me-Time Myth Buster

Let's bust a myth right here: Taking time for yourself doesn't mean you're neglecting your friendships. In fact, when you take a step back and recharge, you're actually making yourself a better, more present friend. Healthy friendships are like a well-balanced circuit—sometimes you need to plug in, and sometimes you need to unplug and let yourself reboot.

Self-Care Isn't Selfish: Saying No with Grace

Ever feel guilty for turning down plans because you just need a night off? It's not about *rejecting* your friends. You are allowed to prioritize yourself. It's about preserving your energy so you can show up for them fully when *you* are ready. So next time you need a break, just say, "I'm in low-power mode right now. Let's hang out next week!" Your real friends will get it.

The Art of the Social Recharge

There are definitely moments when I find myself teetering on the edge of social burnout, and it happens more than I'd like to admit. It usually sneaks up on me during those stretches when I've been saying *yes* to everything—birthday brunches, kids' sporting events, late-night phone calls, spontaneous coffee runs—you name it, I'm there. My social calendar starts to fill up like I'm campaigning for office, with little time left for myself.

Then it hits me. After weeks of constantly showing up for everyone else, I realize I haven't had a single moment to just *be*. I'm drained, snippy, and my battery is flashing dangerously low. That's when I know it's time to take a step back and recharge.

In those moments, I do something counterintuitive—I say no. It's hard when I politely decline the next invite in favor of a much-needed reboot. I spend an entire weekend curled up with a book, binging a show no one else is watching (because let's be real, sometimes you need something you don't have to talk about with anyone). I face-mask, I try to nap (I am a terrible napper!), I do whatever it takes to fill my own cup.

When my friends ask if I'm okay, I just tell them, "I'm in low-power mode right now, so I'll be recharged for our next adventure." And you know what? Friends get it. No guilt trips, no hard feelings. By the time I reconnect with them, I'm back to being my best self—recharged, re-energized, and ready for all the fun and deep conversations. That's when I truly understand that balancing friendship and me-time isn't just necessary—it makes me a better friend in the long run.

Charge Up without the FOMO

- **Create a Me-Time Charging Routine:** Just like your phone has a charger, you need one too. Schedule specific times in your week to recharge, whether it's through reading, journaling, or doing nothing at all. Protect this time as you would a lunch date. You wouldn't cancel on a friend, so don't cancel on yourself!

- **Airplane-Mode Your Social Life:** Not available to hang out? No problem. Send a thoughtful text or a witty one liner to show you are still thinking of them. It's like sending a *low-battery* notification—you're still connected, just on a break.

- **Check Your Battery Levels:** After every social interaction, do a quick self-check. Are you feeling recharged, or are you heading toward low battery? If socializing is draining your energy more often than not, it's time to re-evaluate how much you are giving vs. how much you're saving for yourself.

- **Communicate Openly:** When you need to tap out for some alone time, be upfront. Tell your friends you're not vanishing into thin air—you're just charging up so you can be the best friend possible. Most misunderstandings happen when communication breaks down, so keep it clear and guilt-free.

- **Learn the Art of Saying "No" without Explaining:** Remember, you don't need to write a novel explaining why you can't make it to Saturday's farmers' market. A simple, "I can't this time, but I'm excited for our next hangout!" is all you need. (I am the queen of over-explaining, so this is a skill I'm still working on!)

- **Normalize Personal Time:** Encourage your friends to take breaks too! Let them know it's totally cool to recharge on their own time. Send them a quick message like, "Hey, take care of yourself—I'll be here when you're ready to catch up again."

Just like your favorite devices, you need downtime to perform at your best. Balancing your social life with personal time isn't about dropping out—it's about ensuring you've got enough juice to be fully present when it counts. Remember, you are your own best friend, and taking time for yourself isn't just a luxury; it's a necessity. Don't feel bad about stepping back from your social calendar now and then. Recharge, refresh, and come back to your friendships with a full battery—and maybe a little more sparkle. (And I love some sparkle!) After all, when you're glowing from within, you bring more joy to those around you.

6

ENGAGE FULLY
Let's Talk About Ditching Distractions!

Now that you're all recharged and ready to go, it's time to make sure you're *fully* present when you're with your friends. In today's tech-crazy world, distractions are like uninvited guests at a party—they just show up, grab all your snacks, and make it impossible to focus. From your phone buzzing like it's got the latest hot gossip to that email you just *have* to check, it's easy to get lost in the digital chaos. But when it comes to friendships, these distractions can leave your friend feeling like they are playing second fiddle to your phone.

The Constant Battle for Attention

Whether you are grabbing coffee with a friend or catching up on FaceTime, distractions sneak in like they've got a VIP pass. Maybe your phone lights up with a notification, or you get tempted by the pull of a quick social media scroll while your friend is sharing something important. Think you are great at multitasking? Even if you *think* you're paying attention, half-focused conversations lead to half-baked connections. So, the next time you're with a friend, try to put the phone down and keep your head in the game—because every moment you're truly present is a win for the relationship.

Ever been mid-story, laying out the drama of your week, only to hear, "Wait, check out this TikTok I just got?" It's the friendship equivalent of fumbling the ball right at the goal line. The moment's vibe goes flat, and suddenly, your story is on the sidelines, while the main action happens elsewhere.

All In: Why Showing Up Matters

When you are fully present with a friend—no phone, no interruptions—you are basically giving them a gold medal of attention. In a world where everyone's fighting for attention like it's the final seconds of a championship game, being fully engaged says, 'You're my star player right now.' It's the ultimate move that shows your friends they're worth shutting out all the noise.

The Challenge of Disconnecting

I know it's not easy to hit *Do Not Disturb* in a world where our phones are like an extension of our hands. If you want to strengthen your relationships, sometimes you've got to put your phone in the penalty box and make the person in front of you the main event.

Ask for Presence When It Matters

If you're someone who values deep conversations, and not just surface-level chat, don't hesitate to kindly ask for your friend's full attention. It's not rude—it's more like saying, "Hey, this moment matters, let's be fully here together." A simple, "Can we put our phones down? I really want to talk," can shift the vibe. It's like pressing mute on the outside noise and creating a moment where it's just the two of you, fully present, no distractions—just real, meaningful connection.

Silent Connection Killer: When Distractions Steal the Moment

Now, I'll be the first to admit I am not a saint. There have been plenty of times when I'm wrapped up in something else and only half-listening. But this particular situation made me more aware of just how much it matters to be fully present in a conversation. It was a wake-up call that really opened my eyes to the unintentional effect distractions can have.

I was on the phone with a friend, opening up about a troubling situation with one of my kids. I'd been awake all night, researching ways to help them. I was feeling incredibly vulnerable as I shared with her what was on my heart. As I poured out the details, my phone was buzzing with Instagram notifications, but I ignored it, thinking it wasn't important. Then, in the middle of a sentence my friend interrupted me— "Hold on, I've got to answer this text." The kicker? I found out later my friend was texting one of our other friends while we were knee deep in a heartfelt moment! I immediately switched the subject because I just didn't have the energy to keep sharing after that.

When we hung up, I checked my notifications—and wouldn't you know it? All those Instagram alerts were from her. She'd been sending me posts while I was exposing my raw emotions. It stung, and it made me reflect on my own behavior. I've definitely had moments where I've been the distracted one, but this experience really drove home the importance of giving my friends my full attention.

So, what's the takeaway here? When someone's opening up, put the phone down and *be there*. Even the smallest distractions can unintentionally hurt the people we care about. And trust me the Instagram posts will still be there when the conversation is over.

Stay Present: Simple Moves for Quality Time

- **Phone-Free Time:** When you're with a friend, put your phone away like you're tucking it in for a nap. Seriously, just let it rest. Create intentional, tech-free moments where you can truly be present and show up for each other.

- **Set Boundaries with Technology:** If your phone keeps dinging you like a bad ref, set clear boundaries. Flip it face down or throw it in *Do Not Disturb* mode so you can actually engage.

- **Check in with Yourself:** If our mind starts wandering like it's on a day trip, reel it back in. Breathe, refocus, and if you zoned out, just be honest—your friend will appreciate you snapping back into the conversation.

- **Lead by Example:** Suggest a *phone-free* hangout. You will be amazed at how deep the conversations go when everyone's not sneaking a peek at their screen. Think of it as a workout for your connection, where each screen-free hangout makes your friendship stronger!

Being present isn't just about serious heart-to-heart convos; sometimes it's about chilling in comfortable silence or sharing a laugh without constantly checking the score (ahem, notifications). Whether it's a deep conversation or just hanging out, being fully there shows you are all in. It's like playing a pick-up game where no one's keeping track and everyone is simply enjoying the time together.

STRAIGHT TALK
No Filters, Just Friendships

We know, and hear all the time, that communication is key in romantic relationships. In my romantic relationship, communication is the one thing we talk about *all* the time. We're always working on understanding each other's language whether that means recognizing when one of us feels unheard or knowing when to ask, "Are we even on the same page here?" Why don't we take more time to think about it in our friendships? Friendships require the same level of care and intentionality. I've had moments where I thought I was having a genuine conversation, only to realize my words were just background noise. You know those times when you're sharing a story, and instead of engaging, your friend's response is completely off-topic? It can feel like you're speaking into a void, like your thoughts didn't quite land. It's a reminder that listening isn't just about hearing—it's about being present and truly absorbing what's being said. And that's where intentional communication comes in. It's more than just hearing the words; it's about grasping the meaning beneath them. In friendships, as in romance, communication is the thread that holds it all together, and it's time we treated it that way.

There's a deep longing in humanity to be understood, to build meaningful bonds, and sometimes fear holds us back. I remember when I was going through my divorce, feeling like my entire world had been turned upside down. I was uncomfortable opening up about it, because a part of me wished my friends could just read my mind and know how much I was hurting. I found myself wondering, 'Is it okay to get this deep with my best friends?' The temptation to hide behind passive-aggressive hints or just stay silent was real, hoping maybe they'd somehow figure it out. The truth is that none of us are mind readers. My partner came up with, "Don't Scooby-Doo me," and it's become a playful and pointed reminder to ditch the mystery act. Now it's our way of saying, "Come on, be real with me. What's actually bothering you?" Because passive-aggression only creates distance. If we want real strength in our friendships, we need to drop the guessing games and let ourselves be vulnerable, even when it's hard.

If we're aiming for those authentic connections, it's not just about being vulnerable. It's also about knowing how to communicate with our friends in a way that resonates with them. Part of growing closer is learning that friendship isn't one-size-fits-all. Each person responds differently, and understanding how to approach someone is just as important as what you say. And sometimes, that means knowing when and how to offer feedback.

I've given and received unsolicited advice, and here's what I've learned: I want the friend who tells me, "Hey, that's not really the best color for you," or who makes me pause and reflect before making a big decision. I've also realized that how the feedback is delivered makes all the difference. When it's wrapped in humor and love, it feels supportive, and I can take it in without shutting down. But when it's blunt or harsh, it stings, and I find myself pulling away. It's a delicate balance to strike and it all comes down to knowing how to communicate in a way that truly connects.

On the flip side, I know I've given feedback in ways that weren't wrapped in love, and afterward, I'd feel that gut-wrenching regret, wondering if I could've handled that better. I think we've all been there, where the intention was good, but the delivery fell flat, leaving us wishing we could take it back. That's why it's so important to consider what we're saying, *and* how we're saying it. Sometimes we need to ask ourselves, "Does this really need to be said, or am I nitpicking?" Part of being a good friend is knowing when to let things slide. Feedback should strengthen a friendship, not tear it down, and when it's not coming from a place of love, it can do more harm than good.

And then there's conflict—oh boy. I've seen friendships fall apart because friends didn't have the tools to handle disagreements. It's funny how in romantic relationships, we're all about "working through it," but in friendships, we're sometimes quicker to bail, only to look back later and realize it was probably something small. Disagreements don't have to be the end. They can be opportunities to grow closer—if we're willing to work through them with honesty and humility.

When we face conflict with a friend, it's easy to feel defensive or hurt, and sometimes, walking away feels like the safest option. But the truth is, disagreements can reveal so much about a friendship—how strong it is, how willing we are to grow, and how deeply we care. It's in those tough moments that we have a chance to be real with each other. Yes, it's uncomfortable, and sometimes it feels easier to brush things under the rug, which only leaves room for resentment to build.

It's worth asking, "What's more important, being right or preserving the relationship?" When we let our guard down and approach conflict with an open heart—acknowledging our part in it and being willing to listen—we create space for understanding. That's a connection that strengthens over time. It's like pulling weeds in a garden. It might be hard work, but once the conflict is resolved then your friendship is primed to grow with even stronger roots.

Of course, not every friendship stands the test of time. There are moments when the issue at hand reveals a deeper incompatibility. More often than not, small misunderstandings turn into bigger problems simply because we avoid having the tough conversations. If we approach conflict as a way to better understand each other, it becomes a bridge to stronger friendships, not a roadblock. And when we handle it with grace, we show our friends that they are worth the effort.

In this section, we're going to explore all of these dynamics. How can we communicate in ways that deepen our friendships, make us feel heard, and create space for vulnerability? How can we offer and receive feedback without hurting each other? And most importantly, how can we navigate disagreements in a way that strengthens, rather than breaks, our bonds? That Inner Circle is worth the effort, and the best ones are built on the kind of communication that brings us closer, even when it's hard.

COMMUNICATION
The Dance of Connection

Communication in friendships isn't just about exchanging words—it's about tuning in. Think of communication like dancing, syncing with your partner and moving with a purpose, not just going through the motions. If you're only hearing the words and missing the feelings behind them, you're not dancing to the same beat.

Listening with Intention: Feeling the Rhythm

You know that moment when someone says, "I hear you," but you know they're just going through the steps without feeling the music? That's what happens when you don't listen with intention. Real listening is when you catch the beat in a dance—you're not just waiting to take your turn; you're tuning into the flow. It's when you pause, lean in, and say, "Tell me more about that," instead of jumping in with your own response.

Emotional Awareness: Reading the Moves

In dancing, it's not just about your own steps—you are reading the whole dance floor. Same with conversations—it's not just the words, it's how they're said. Your friend might say, "I'm fine," but their posture or tone tells you they're anything but. That's your cue to step in with emotional support, offering a compassionate ear or a validating word. And if you're talking on the phone, ask if they'd like to FaceTime. It's like getting a clearer view of the dance, where you can catch subtle shifts in emotion and body language. If FaceTime isn't their thing, no worries, respect that. The point is, offering that deeper connection shows you are committed to the Tango.

Empathy: Finding the Rhythm of Support

When you tune into your partner's rhythm, that's where you find empathy—it's about sensing when to step forward and when to let your friend take the lead. When a friend is struggling, sometimes simply acknowledging their feelings with, "I can see why that's tough," can feel like offering them the perfect spin. Empathy isn't about relating your own experience, it's holding space for theirs. Instead of saying, "I know exactly how you feel," try "I've been through something similar, and I'd love to hear more about what you're going through." It's their moment to express themselves, and empathy allows you to offer support without stepping into the spotlight, keeping their story front and center.

Clarification: Avoid Stepping on Toes
Ever been on a dance floor, unsure of the next move, and ended up stepping on someone's toes? That's what it feels like when you misunderstand a conversation. If things get confusing, it's better to pause and clarify rather than stumble ahead. Ask questions or try paraphrasing to make sure you're both on the same page, just like a well-timed pause in a dance routine ensures you're in sync before going on. You're saying, you care enough to get this right.

Responding Thoughtfully: Don't Rush the Moves
Sometimes, you need to slow down and let your friend take the lead. It's not about fast moves or quick responses. By giving them space to express themselves fully, you're showing them you're here for the whole dance, not just the highlights. It sends the message, "I respect you enough to hear everything before I jump in." If your friend opens up, don't feel the need to rush in and reply. Take your time, like waiting for the perfect beat before making your next move. Thoughtful responses show that you're not just reacting for the sake of it; you're considering their words and aiming for a meaningful, intentional reply. Sometimes, saying, "I need a moment to process this," is the best move you can make.

When Friends Truly Listen: Support Beyond Words
There was a time when I was really struggling with my health, particularly after having my thyroid removed. My thyroid levels were dangerously high, and I was terrified of what that meant for my body and my well-being. On top of that, no matter what I did, I couldn't seem to lose the weight that had piled on, which sent me into a spiral of self-doubt and depression. I had opened up to a few friends about it, and while they were sympathetic, the responses were more like passing remarks: "Oh yeah, I've heard of that" or "I had something similar happen once." I didn't blame them, but those comments felt like they skimmed the surface of what I was going through, and it made me feel even more isolated in my experience.

Then there was Charlotte. She didn't just acknowledge my words and move on—she leaned all the way in. She looked at me with genuine concern and asked for more details. She wanted to understand how I was feeling, physically and emotionally. When I explained the fear and frustration I felt, Charlotte didn't just nod or offer quick fixes. She asked follow-up questions about my symptoms, how they were affecting my day-to-day life, and how I was really holding up beneath it all.

She took the time to listen and even shared that she had a client at work with similar health struggles, but instead of making the conversation about someone else, she made it clear she was fully focused on me. And then she went even further—researching homeopathic remedies and potential dietary options that could help alleviate some of my symptoms. Every time we talked, she checked in on my upcoming doctor's appointments, reminding me that I wasn't alone in this and that she cared about what was happening to me, not just as a casual listener but as someone deeply invested in my well-being.

It wasn't just about Charlotte giving advice or trying to fix my situation. What made the difference was how fully present she was. She was there with me in the trenches, willing to help carry my burden and making sure I knew she had my back. She didn't just let me offload my worries—she held them with me, which gave me the emotional strength I needed to keep pushing through.

Her presence, her attentiveness, and her compassion made all the difference. Charlotte reminded me that true communication isn't just about hearing words—it's about actively listening, processing the words and walking alongside someone through the tough stuff. That's the essence of a strong bond.

The Rhythm of Friendship: Mastering Communication Moves

- **Create Active Listening Zones:** Like a spotlight on the dance floor, give your full attention during important conversations. Whether over coffee or on a walk, practice letting those moments be all about intentional listening.

- **Know Their Communication Style:** Just like dance styles, every friend has their unique way of connecting. Some are all about quick and direct texts, while others prefer lengthy, intimate sit-downs. Some friends need space to think before responding, while others respond immediately, keeping the energy flowing. Then there are friends who connect best through humor, preferring playful exchanges over serious discussions, and others who lean into reflective, in–depth conversations. Matching these styles—whether it's light banter, practical check ins, or meaningful face-to-face moments—keeps the connection strong.

- **Ask for Their Needs:** After a tough conversation, hit them with a "What do you need from me right now?" It's like offering to lead or follow in the dance—letting them decide how you can best support them and giving them options for how you can help.

So, next time you're in a conversation, think of it like a dance. Tune in to your partner, listen for the rhythm, and move with intention. When you show up with empathy, curiosity, and patience, you're not just hearing words—you're dancing your way to a deeper, more connected friendship!

SCOOBY CLUES NOT NEEDED
Let's Get Direct About Support

Even the best dance moves won't save you if your partner in the routine isn't sharing what's on their mind. You know those moments when you wish your besties could just read your mind, like you're sending out psychic signals through your intense eye contact? Yeah, I've been there too. But here's the scoop—unless your friend is secretly part of the Scooby-Doo gang with mystery-solving abilities, they probably can't guess *exactly* what you need. Expecting people to know when you're struggling without a word is like expecting Scooby-Doo to solve a case without snacks—it's not happening!

We've all been in that situation where we're silently hoping our friends will swoop in like the Mystery Machine rolling up just in time, but sadly they're not cruising around with psychic powers. Skip the mystery and just ask for what you need. It's that simple.

Imagine how much smoother life would be if, instead of sending out vague telepathic signals, you just said, "Hey, I need help." Or even better, "Could you bring some treats and listen to me vent for 10 minutes?" Clear, direct, and no dog detective required. This way, you're not only expressing your needs, you're also giving your friends a clear way to show up for you.

No Crystal Balls Needed
Asking for support doesn't make you a burden; it makes you human. Do you expect your friends to just know what's wrong? If yes, that's setting them up for failure, like sending Scooby into a haunted house without Shaggy. Instead, being open and direct about your needs is like giving them a map to help you out of your funk.

The next time you're feeling overwhelmed, don't just hope someone reads your mind. Be proactive. Say something like, "I could really use your advice—can we talk for a bit?" or "I'm having a rough day, any chance we can hang out?" You're not only making things easier for your friends, but you are also building stronger, deeper connections in the process.

Ruh Roh! Spotting Clues When Friends Are Struggling

My girlfriend Joanne and I talk nearly every day, so when she landed a new job she was really excited about, I was thrilled for her. The pay was better, the growth opportunities looked promising, and the work was something she could really sink her teeth into. But about six months in, I noticed something was off. She didn't seem her usual, bubbly self, but whenever I asked how things were going, she'd shrug it off and say, "Oh, just busy."

Weeks went by, and one day I finally asked her directly, "Joanne, what's really going on at work? You don't seem like yourself." She hesitated for a moment before opening up, sharing that her boss was making her work six long days a week, calling her after hours, and creating a generally hostile work environment. She felt trapped and unsure of what to do.

For weeks, we brainstormed, putting our heads together to create an exit plan that would allow her to transition to something she loved without losing the financial stability she needed. I was so glad she finally let her guard down, and it also made me realize how long she'd been suffering in silence. As her best friend, I wished she hadn't waited so long to reach out for help, and I also understood that everyone comes to these moments in their own time.

This experience reminded me how important it is to check in with our friends—and to let them know it's okay to ask for support before they reach their breaking point. We often think that our friends are strong enough to handle it all, though even the strongest people need someone in their corner, ready to offer a hand when things get overwhelming. Joanne's situation showed me that no one should ever feel like they have to carry the weight of the world on their own, especially when they have friends who are more than willing to help lighten the load.

Now, I make it a point to be more proactive in my friendships—asking the extra "Are you really okay?" Sometimes all it takes is a gentle nudge to remind someone that they don't have to struggle alone. Isn't that what friends are for? And just like the Scooby-Doo gang never leaves a mystery unsolved, we shouldn't leave our friends' struggles hidden either. So pull off the mask, offer support, and make sure no one has to face life's challenges alone—even if there aren't any spooky ghosts involved!

Scooby Clues Not Required

- **Be Direct & Clear:** Your friends aren't detectives, so give them the scoop! "I've been feeling stressed and need to talk." Easy. Now they know exactly what to do without fumbling through clues.

- **Start Small:** If asking for help feels like jumping into the deep end, dip a toe in first. Try "Can you give me feedback on this text?" You'll find that asking for help doesn't need to feel like chasing down a runaway sandwich with the Scooby gang.

- **Encourage Two-Way Support:** Once you have asked for what you need, flip the script. Ask, "I've been leaning on you—what can I do for you?" Friendships work best when we're unmasking villains together, offering mutual support.

- **Collaborate on Boundaries:** Are you asking for too much? It's totally okay to check in—"Is this too much for you right now?" It keeps communication clear and respectful. Nobody wants to feel like Velma carrying all the clues.

Like anything else, asking for help takes practice. At first, it might feel like Scooby trying to walk on two legs—wobbly and weird. But trust me, the more you do it, the more natural it becomes. Asking for support isn't awkward; it's empowering! It's what makes friendships extraordinarily strong, just like teamwork in unraveling a mystery. So ditch the mind-reading act, drop the guessing games, and make your friendships even stronger by being real about what you need.

9

TIMING IS EVERYTHING
When to Give Your Friend the 411

Of course, asking for support is only one side of the coin. Sometimes, friendship also means being the one who speaks up—especially when your friend needs a little tough love. But how do you know when to speak up and give your friend an opinion they might not want to hear? Is it when they're rocking those neon leggings that make them look like a highlighter? Or when they're about to dive headfirst into a questionable relationship?

It's a fine line to walk. Offer your opinion too early, and you risk coming off as critical. Say nothing, and you might watch your friend wade through unnecessary drama. So, how do we find the balance between friendly advice and the bigger revelations? Let's break down when to share those helpful nuggets of wisdom (gently, of course) and when it's best to just pass the remote.

Quick Saves: Fashion, Fun & Friendly Advice

We've all been there—your friend's about to do something that has *bad idea* written all over it in bold, flashing lights. Maybe it's something lighthearted, like when they're sporting an outfit that looks like they just raided a 1993 time capsule. Or perhaps it's something more serious, like quitting their job on a whim because their boss chewed them out for their report formatting.

Think of these as the casual moments where a quick, honest comment can save the day. Whether its fashion advice or a poorly timed hobby decision, these moments don't always have life-altering consequences. Maybe your friend wants to try karaoke after a few cocktails and insists they've got Mariah Carey–level talent (in case you are wondering, they don't). Here, a well-placed, "Maybe let's save the whistle notes for another time," could prevent a minor social disaster. For other situations you can use lines like: "Would you like my honest opinion on this outfit?" Or maybe, "You always rock bold looks—want me to help you find something that's just as fab but shows off how sensational you are?"

Big Life Decisions: Channel Your Inner Mr. Miyagi

Then there are the moments where your friend is about to make a choice that could change the trajectory of their life. Should you jump in? Absolutely—this is where you go from sidekick to trusted advisor, like the friend who yanks them out of the path of an oncoming metaphorical bus. The trick is doing so gently that they don't feel attacked. You want to be more Yoda than drill sergeant. Maybe say: "I admire your ambition, but have you thought through a plan B if things don't go as expected?" Or "I have noticed a few things, and I'm worried about how this might play out. Can we talk about it?"

When to Step In (without Looking Like the Fun Police)

Now, before you start spraying feedback like a garden hose, take a second to think: Is this the right moment? Check the weather—your friend's emotional weather, that is. Are they already having a Category 5 meltdown, or are they open and relaxed, like a sunny beach day? Timing is everything in these situations.

Maybe your friend is diving into a new romance, and you're tempted to ask: "I love that you're happy, but are you sure you're ready for the next step so soon?" However, sometimes your friend is just looking for validation, not a TED Talk on the pros and cons of their current relationship choices.

If they're having a low-stakes moment (like picking an Instagram filter), maybe don't drop hard truths about how that filter is going to make them look like they've been living under a fluorescent light for a decade. But, if it's a deeper conversation and your friend says, "I need your honest opinion," that's your cue to pull out the big guns—but make sure you've got a safety net of compassion to soften the blow.

Ask what they need before jumping into the conversation. Try this: "Do you want to talk it out, or would you rather I just listen?" Sometimes, your friend needs to vent without hearing solutions. Other times, they're seeking your wisdom, so let them decide.

Strike the Right Chord: Mastering Balanced Feedback

Offering tough feedback is like tuning a guitar—too tight, and the string snaps; too loose, and there's no harmony. You want just the right amount of tension for harmony. When your friend is about to make a major life decision (like moving to a new city on a whim, ya that was me), a well-placed, "Have you thought about XYZ?" can go a long way. Keep it calm and offer suggestions instead of commands, unless you want it to feel like an intervention straight out of a reality show.

Throwing Shade or Sharing Insight? It's All About Delivery

Giving feedback doesn't mean you need to be a stand-up comedian or a life coach but the delivery, it's crucial. It's all in the wrapping paper. If you've got a hard piece of advice to deliver, wrap it up with kindness, maybe even a joke. "Hey, I love you to the moon and back, but maybe we retire those pants until the next '90s party."

If you're too blunt, you risk creating tension. If you sugarcoat it too much, they might not take it seriously. Somewhere in the middle lies the perfect balance—like getting your coffee just right—not too bitter, not too sweet.

How to Keep Feedback a Collaborative Process

Sometimes giving feedback feels like dropping a live grenade. Remember, this is a conversation, not a one-person show. Encourage your friend to give you their perspective. Maybe there's more to their story that you didn't know about. "I get where you're coming from but tell me more about what's making you feel this way," can be a magical phrase. It shows you care about hearing their side, and not just about doling out advice.

Follow-Through, Not Just Follow-Up

After a tough conversation, don't let it float away like a helium balloon. Follow up later. "I've been thinking about our conversation. How's everything going with that decision?" This shows you're invested in their well-being, and not just tossing advice from a distance.

Tactful Timing: Sharing Tough News, One-on-One

My girlfriend Andrea and I both left our hometown of Seattle on the same day—her heading to Texas, and me to Arizona. We've stayed close despite the distance, and recently she called me in tears. She'd been juggling long hours at work, managing two young kids with jam-packed sports schedules, and always has a home remodeling project on the go. She was excited to take a break and go to a local fall festival with some new neighborhood friends.

What should have been a fun afternoon became an overwhelming, emotional ordeal. While enjoying the afternoon with her new friends, one of the ladies suddenly leaned in and commented on how Andrea's clothes smelled. The woman said they had a musty, moldy odor—like they'd been left in the washer too long. Andrea, who takes great pride in keeping her clothes clean, was embarrassed but tried to brush it off, explaining that the clothes were freshly washed. Yet, the friend wouldn't let it go. She even went so far as to physically smell Andrea's clothes again in front of everyone, continuing to comment and questioning if Andrea knew how to clean her washer.

Andrea was mortified. She tried to steer the conversation away, but the woman just kept pressing. This is the perfect example of when, maybe, instead of publicly nitpicking, you pull your friend aside and gently share your concerns privately. Some insights are better served with compassion and discretion, especially when they're about something as personal as cleanliness. In situations like this, the goal is to maintain your friend's dignity while addressing the issue—because even well-meaning honesty can sting when it's dished out in front of an audience.

Mindful Moments: Offering Honest Feedback with Care

- **Silent Reflection:** Ask yourself, "Will this matter in six months?" If it's a minor blip on the radar, let it go. But if it's the equivalent of a slow-motion train wreck, offer your words gently, like delivering bad news with a glass of Pinot Grigio.

- **Check the Timing:** Timing is everything. If they're in a moment of excitement or celebration, maybe hold off on the heavy feedback. If it's a serious conversation, go for it—with caution.

- **Ask Before You Dive In:** Before unloading your thoughts, ask if they're open to hearing feedback. A simple, "Do you want advice or just to vent?" can prevent a lot of misunderstandings.

- **Sandwich Method for Big Decisions:** Start with something positive, offer your feedback, then end with reassurance. For example, "I love that you're excited about this move. Have you considered XYZ? But I know you've got great instincts, and whatever you decide, I've got your back."

- **Give Them Space to Think:** After offering your input, don't hover or pressure. Give them the space to process it and come back to you when they're ready.

- **Personal Reflection:** Try journaling or reflecting after your conversations. Were there moments where you jumped in too soon? Did your friend seem relieved or overwhelmed? Tracking your patterns can help you refine your approach.

Being a good friend doesn't mean biting your tongue, and it also doesn't mean going full-on truth serum every chance you get. Whether it's a wardrobe malfunction or a life-altering decision, finding the right balance between gentle honesty and full-blown intervention is key. Sometimes the best way to support your friends is to speak up. Other times, it's about handing them the mic and listening.

So next time you're wondering whether to drop wisdom or stay quiet, just remember you're not here to solve every problem. You're here to be a friend, and friends sometimes offer reality checks with a side of humor, and maybe a big glass of wine.

10

BEYOND SMALL TALK
The Power of Genuine Feedback

Delivering feedback is only half the battle. Sometimes, the real challenge begins afterward—what happens when that well-intended comment isn't received like a warm hug but more like a cold splash of water? What do you do when you hit a wall of resistance, defensiveness, or—worse—radio silence?

While sharing insights is an essential part of friendship, managing the reaction can feel like juggling flaming torches—tricky, delicate, and a bit risky. Not every friend is ready for feedback, and not every perspective is easily accepted. So, what do you do when your well-intended insight lands with the grace of a piano falling from a second-story window?

When the Fun Fades: Facing Tough Conversations
Some friends are as allergic to feedback as cats are to water. Maybe they shut down, go silent, or throw up a defensive shield the moment something they don't want to hear sneaks into the conversation. Being a good friend means sometimes speaking up, even when it feels like stepping on Legos barefoot. The challenge? Knowing when your opinion really matters and when it's okay to let them live in their Legoland. But here's the kicker (and yes, I know I'm driving this point home): Too much silence can crack the foundation of your friendship. If you never speak up about the big stuff—like their impulsive decision to quit their job and become a llama farmer—they might start wondering if you're really paying attention or just playing the role of a overly bystander.

When Words Sting: Giving Space After Tough Talks
We've all been there: You offer a nugget of wisdom, expecting a *Thank you*, and instead, you're met with the emotional equivalent of a closed door. It's like trying to pet a cat that's not in the mood—no matter how gentle you are, you're going to get scratched.

When your friend gets defensive, avoid playing emotional tug-of-war. Stay calm, back off, and give them room to process. Sometimes, they just need a moment to cool off and get back to their happy place before revisiting the topic.

Understanding Resistance: Why Some Friends Resist the Feedback

Navigating these moments is like trying to win a game of dodgeball—You have to understand why your friend is dodging your feedback. It's rarely about what you said, it could be about insecurities, past heartbreaks, or maybe they're just in a slump. Think of critique like the sun—for some, it's warm and welcome. For others, it's overexposure that sends them scrambling for the nearest shade.

When Friends Ghost: The Vanishing Act After Tough Talks

Sometimes, after sharing hard-to-hear perceptions, your friend might disappear faster than a shooting star. It's frustrating, but yes, some people need time to process. Heartfelt insights can take a while to settle, so the fallout isn't always immediate. In these moments, give them space to sift through their feelings without chasing them down with a megaphone asking, "Are we okay?!"

A gentle follow-up later can reopen the door to the conversation. "I've been thinking about our chat. How are you feeling about it now?" let them know you care without sending out a search party.

Respecting Their Journey

Sometimes, no matter how delicately you present your thoughts, your friend just isn't open to hearing them. Maybe they don't want to hear your opinion on their latest fling or career detour, and you have to respect that. At some point, it's their life, their decisions, and their potential mess to clean up.

Even if you're watching them sail into stormy seas, remember—you're not their captain. You're the supportive friend on shore with a towel and a cup of tea for when they get back. Let them live their journey, even if you're tempted to commandeer their ship.

Restitching the Friendship

If your feedback caused a rift, don't assume the friendship is over. Time—and maybe a little humor—can mend the gap. Send the occasional check in, remind them you're still there, and when they're ready, rebuild the connection over a shared laugh or coffee. Picture it like mending a stitch that's come undone—you may have pulled the thread too tight, but with care, you can sew things back together.

The Gentle Nudge: Speaking Up When It's Tough

I have a friend named Laura, and if there's one thing you can say about her, it's that she's a force of nature. She's the type of person who dives headfirst into everything—whether it's her career, her personal goals, or supporting the people she loves. That go-all-in attitude was something I admired about her from the start. But as life picked up speed for both of us, I started noticing cracks in that relentless energy she always had. There were times she'd show up late to our plans, bags under her eyes, clearly exhausted. At first, I didn't say anything because, hey, who am I to tell her how to live her life? But as time went on, it became harder to ignore the toll it was taking.

She was constantly juggling more than any one person should—leading projects at work, organizing charity events, managing family responsibilities—and I could see her running on fumes. It was like watching someone drive a car with the gas gage on low, refusing to pull over. The thing is, Laura's the type who prided herself on handling everything, so I hesitated to bring it up. Then one day, after one too many rushed conversations and seeing her spread so thin, I knew I couldn't just watch it happen anymore.

We were having lunch at one of our usual spots, and something in her demeanor that day struck me—she was there with me, but I could tell her mind was racing. She was tapping her phone non-stop, checking emails, planning out her afternoon, and it hit me that she hadn't been truly *in the moment* for a while. I figured if I didn't say something now, I'd regret it.

When we finished eating, I leaned in and said, "Laura, I've been noticing how much you've been juggling lately, and I'm really worried about you. You're amazing at handling everything, but I'm afraid you're running yourself into the ground."

As soon as the words left my mouth, I could see her entire body tense up. It was like I had pulled a lever, and a defensive wall shot up between us. She put down her phone, gave me this tight-lipped smile, and said, "I'm fine. I always manage. I don't need anyone worrying about me or telling me how to live my life."

The coldness in her response caught me off guard. I was coming from a place of care, but it was clear Laura saw it as me questioning her ability to handle her own life. I didn't push it any further, and the conversation left a lingering awkwardness between us. Over the next few weeks, we didn't talk much, and when we did, it was politely distant. I started second-guessing myself, wondering if I had overstepped, or if I should've just kept quiet and let her figure things out on her own.

For months, things stayed that way—polite, surface-level, and a little strained. Then, one afternoon, out of nowhere, I got a text from Laura. It was simple: "Hey, I've been thinking a lot about what you said. I wasn't ready to hear it at the time, but I'm really glad you said something."

I can't explain the relief that washed over me. We met up not long after, and she opened up about how overwhelmed she'd been. She admitted that, deep down, she knew she was running on empty but saying it out loud made it feel too real, too hard to admit. She thanked me for being the one to call it out, even if she hadn't been ready to hear it. It was like that conversation had planted a seed, and though it took time, it eventually led her to reassess and slow down.

What struck me the most was how in the end speaking up, actually brought us closer. Once she got past her initial defensiveness, Laura realized that my words, though tough to hear, came from a place of love. It wasn't about pointing out her flaws or telling her what to do—it was about caring enough to say something when I saw she was struggling.

This experience taught me that sometimes, even when the feedback feels uncomfortable, it's necessary. Not every friend will be ready to handle it in the moment, and that's okay. The important part is that you cared enough to share it, and in time, that insight can become the catalyst for deeper connection and growth.

Strengthening Bonds After Tough Talks

- **Give Them Space:** If your friend ghosts you after a tough conversation, take a deep breath and give them time to process. It's important to resist the urge to bombard them with messages or call them repeatedly, as this might add to their stress. Instead, let them know you're there when they're ready to talk. A simple message like, "I'm here if you need me," can reassure them without pressure. They'll come back when they're ready—hopefully, with their emotional bags unpacked.

- **Respect Their Choices:** If your friend consistently rejects your advice, it's time to shift to a supportive role. Instead of pushing your perspective, try asking open-ended questions that encourage them to explore their feelings and thoughts. For instance, you might say, "What do you think you want to do next?" This shows that you value their autonomy and are there to listen rather than direct. Let them know you're always there for support, but ultimately, it's their choice to make.

- **Mend the Gap:** Follow up after the dust settles. "I know things were a little tense, but I'd love to chat when you're ready. I miss hanging out with you." Keep it light and sincere. When you do connect, you might also want to acknowledge the previous conversation, focusing on how much you value your friendship and want to understand their feelings.

- **Encourage Openness:** Create a culture of openness in your friendship. At the right moment, express how much you value honest conversations, even the tough ones. You might say something like, "I know we've had some hard talks, but I want you to know that you can always tell me what's on your mind. I promise to listen without judgment." This sets the stage for your friend to feel safe in sharing their thoughts and feelings, knowing that it's a collaborative path.

Navigating the waters of friendship can be a delicate endeavor, much like steering a boat together—each person must guide their way while being mindful not to rock the boat too much. While some friends may not be ready to hear your advice, excessive silence can create barriers where there could be connections. The true art of friendship lies in knowing when to speak up, when to step back, and when to simply share a laugh.

11

DISAGREEMENTS
Don't Have to Be a Disaster!

Even with the closest friends, not every chat is bound to be sunshine and rainbows. Sometimes, disagreements pop up out of nowhere—like an unwelcome zit on picture day. But don't panic! A little conflict isn't the end of the world. In fact, it's an opportunity to learn, grow, and *maybe* come out on the other side with a stronger friendship (and hopefully not a long list of petty insults). So, let's talk about how to handle disagreements with a lot of grace—and maybe a little humor.

Stay Cool, Calm & Collected
I know it's tempting to throw out that perfectly timed, snarky comeback when you're in the heat of the moment (I know, I know, you've been *waiting* to use it). But reacting like you're in a reality TV showdown isn't going to help. Instead, practice *the pause*. It's like hitting the snooze button on your reaction. It gives you time to calm down and *not* say something you'll regret five seconds later.

Listen Like a Pro
It's easy to get stuck in *I'm right, you're wrong* mode. However, disagreements are not about winning; They're about *understanding* the other person's perspective. So instead of going full courtroom drama, ask something like, "Can you explain what you mean by that?" When we listen with curiosity instead of defensiveness, we open the door to a more meaningful conversation, and often, we find common ground we didn't expect. Think of it as hitting the "zoom in" button on Google Earth—suddenly you're not just looking at the map, you're diving into the details. You're not merely exchanging words; you're truly engaging with each other's thoughts and feelings. This shift transforms the conversation from a surface-level exchange into a deeper dialogue, fostering understanding and connection.

Empathy Unlocks Next-Level Friendships
Ever notice how much easier it is to keep your cool when you remember your friend isn't *actually* the villain in your life movie? Empathy is your go-to power move. Instead of seeing them as the *enemy*, picture them

as your partner in solving the problem. When you show empathy, it's like holding a flashlight in the dark—you're illuminating their path and helping them navigate through their feelings.

Empathy lets you see through their lens, even if just for a moment, to understand where they're coming from and why they feel the way they do. You start to see beyond surface reactions, recognizing that they may be dealing with stress, self-doubt, or past experiences that shape how they respond. By letting empathy guide you, you invite them to express thoughts more freely, creating a safe, judgment-free zone.

Words Matter, Choose Them Wisely
Remember that time you said, "You always..." and your friend responded with an Oscar-worthy "Oh really?!?" moment? Let's avoid that. Instead of triggering phrases like "You never," try saying "I feel" or "I noticed." It's a lot less like lighting a match and more like offering a cup of tea. And who can argue over tea?

Compromise without Compromising Yourself
Compromise sounds a little like settling, right? But not here! Find that sweet spot where both of you feel valued and respected—like agreeing to split the last slice of pizza. No one walks away hungry, and no one feels like they lost. Real compromise doesn't mean sacrificing who you are or what you need; it means creating space for both perspectives without giving up your own. When done right, you're not bending so much that you lose your shape—you're finding a solution that brings the two of you closer without losing yourself along the way.

Learn from the Storm
Disagreements aren't just awkward—they are *educational!* After a good old-fashioned squabble, take a moment to ask, "What did I learn about myself or this friendship?" It's like watching the bloopers after a movie—you get to see what went wrong and laugh about it later. Through understanding our triggers and patterns we're able to unlock a key strength for the next time we face a tough conversation.

Turning Tension into Connection
A friend of mine recently shared a story about a disagreement that nearly derailed one of her longest and closest friendships. She and her friend Rachel had known each other for decades and had always seen

eye-to-eye on most things. But there was one topic that had become a bit of a sore spot over the years—politics. They had always managed to sidestep it, keeping their differences at bay in order to avoid conflict. Eventually, the subject came up.

It was during a casual dinner with some mutual friends, and things had been going great until someone brought up the recent election. At first the conversation was light, with a few jokes tossed around. Then Rachel made an offhand comment about a particular political issue, and that's when my friend felt something shift inside her. She didn't even realize how much the issue had been weighing on her—how much it had become a source of internal frustration. Rachel wasn't saying anything overly harsh or offensive, but in the heat of the moment, it felt personal.

Before my friend knew it, she found herself snapping back, throwing her own opinion into the mix with more force than she intended. The energy at the table shifted from friendly banter to palpable tension. The others at the table tried to steer the conversation back to safer ground, but the two of them were already locked in. Each comment felt like an escalating tug-of-war, each trying to prove a point. It didn't feel like a conversation anymore—it felt like a battle, with neither side willing to back down.

By the time the dinner ended, they had both retreated into awkward silence. My friend left feeling frustrated, upset, and a little unsure about what had just happened. She replayed the conversation in her head, frustrated that she had let things get so out of hand. Days passed without either of them reaching out. The longer the silence went on, the more my friend began to wonder if this disagreement had caused permanent damage. She loved Rachel and didn't want to let this conflict fester.

Then, out of the blue Rachel sent her a text: "I feel like our conversation didn't end well. Can we meet and talk it through?"

That message was exactly what my friend needed. They met up a few days later for coffee, and the first thing they did was acknowledge that the conversation had spiraled in a way neither of them intended. Rachel admitted she hadn't realized how sensitive the topic was for my friend and that she had gotten caught up in trying to make her point. My friend, in turn, admitted that she had overreacted and let her emotions get the better of her. They both agreed that while they had strong opinions on this particular topic, they weren't worth damaging their friendship over.

Instead of diving back into the heated debate, they shifted their focus to how the conversation made them feel. They talked about the stress of the current political climate and how it was affecting them in different ways. By focusing on their emotions rather than the disagreement itself, they were able to find common ground. They didn't need to agree on the issue—they needed to understand why the conversation had gotten so intense.

What my friend realized after this conversation was that the disagreement itself wasn't the problem. It was how they handled it. In the moment, they had both been more focused on proving a point than on listening to each other. But once they stepped back, let their guard down, and approached the situation with empathy, they were able to rebuild that bridge.

After that conversation, they were closer than ever and not because they had resolved the political disagreement but because they'd learned how to handle conflict in a way that strengthened their friendship instead of breaking it down. Now, whenever a tense topic comes up, they make it a point to listen more and react less. It's not about being right—it's about valuing the relationship enough to navigate disagreements with respect and care.

This story reminds me of how even the most well-intentioned remarks can sting in the moment. With empathy, patience, and a willingness to see the other person's perspective, it's possible to turn what could be a relationship-ending disagreement into a bonding moment. Disagreements are inevitable in any friendship, but they don't have to end in disaster. Sometimes they are just the opportunity we need to cultivate greater intimacy.

Conflict into Connection: Turning Disagreements into Wins

- **Practice the Pause:** Next time you're about to unleash your inner sass master, take a deep breath, count to five, and ask yourself, "Do I want to resolve this, or just drop a mic?" Pause before you speak—it will save you from unnecessary drama and tense follow-up texts.

- **Step into Their World:** Ask yourself, 'If I were them, how would I feel.' It's like trying on a new pair of glasses—everything looks different, and you have the ability to see things more clearly.

Suddenly, the convo shifts from "I'm right, you're wrong" to "Okay, let's figure this out together."

- **Avoid Absolutes:** Replace "You always" or "You never" with "I feel" or "I've noticed." For example, "I've noticed we've had a few misunderstandings lately. Can we talk about how we're approaching things?"

- **Sharing the Winning Trophy:** Instead of focusing on who's right, ask, "How can we both feel good about this?" Think of it as a way to share the metaphorical pizza of friendship, making sure no one is stuck with the crust.

- **Reflect After the Conflict:** After the dust has settled (and you've hugged it out), ask yourself, "What could I do differently next time?" Cue the drumroll—instant character development!

Disagreements happen. But with a little empathy, a pause button on your reactions, and some well-chosen words, you can turn a potential friendship disaster into an opportunity for growth, and maybe a few laughs.

So next time a disagreement is brewing, remember you've *got* this. Handle it with humor, heart, and a whole lot of respect, and you will come out stronger than before—no reality TV meltdowns required.

THE FRIENDSHIP GLOW-UP
Where Feelings Meet Growth

When I started writing this book, I wrestled with self-doubt. Could I really pull it off? What kept me going—more than anything—was my friends. They encouraged me, celebrated every milestone with me, and reminded me of my own strength when I questioned it. Do you have that one friend who calls you the moment she gets her quarterly bonus, just because she knows you'll be just as excited as she is? Or the friend who says, "I have this idea, what do you think?" and you dive right in, cheering her on as she takes the first steps toward her dream? The essence of true friendship is found in our commitment to stand by each other, offering support and recognizing every achievement, no matter how modest or monumental.

These joyful moments are essential, and when we combine them with a willingness to embrace vulnerability and share our challenges, our friendships become even richer. I've learned that creating a safe space for my friends to share often means I may have to go first, revealing parts of myself I've been afraid to expose. Vulnerability feels risky, though it's the key to deepening our bonds. It shows our friends they're not alone in their struggles, and that kind of openness strengthens the foundation of a friendship.

However, the journey of friendship isn't always clear skies. There are times when mistakes happen and feelings get hurt, and that's where the art of apologizing comes into play. I've had to learn how to apologize with compassion and genuine sincerity, recognizing that it's not just a one-off act but an ongoing commitment to owning my actions and making amends. Forgiveness, too, is a process that requires effort, reminding us that friendships thrive on the care and attention we invest, even when the road gets bumpy.

Acknowledging our missteps and expressing vulnerability not only strengthens our bonds but also lays the groundwork for deeper appreciation. That appreciation is vital; it's the ongoing expressions of love and gratitude that keep our friendships vibrant. I'm the kind of person who lights up from words of affirmation—I'm all about the lovey-dovey stuff and knowing that my inner circle cares for and appreciates me is everything. Growing up, love sometimes felt like it was given and taken away too quickly, so having friends who make me feel valued fills a deep need in me. I've also started practicing gratitude regularly, starting each day with a thankful heart, and it's done wonders for my well-being. That love and gratitude I pour into my friendships has come back tenfold, creating a wave of warmth and camaraderie that enriches everyone around me.

I also have realized how each person plays a distinct role in my life. Every friend contributes a unique perspective, like a collection of puzzle pieces that together help me navigate the ups and downs. Understanding who to turn to for what has been a lifesaver, and it's made me appreciate each friend for what they bring into my world.

Ultimately, the tapestry of friendship is woven from threads of encouragement, vulnerability, compassion, and appreciation. Each element plays a vital role in creating a bond that is resilient and deeply rewarding. As we navigate the complexities of our connections, it's essential to remember that every shared moment, whether joyful or challenging, adds depth and texture to our relationships. By embracing these aspects, we strengthen our friendships and foster a community of support. Let's dive deeper into these themes and explore how they manifest in our daily lives, enriching our experiences and those of our friends.

12

GROWING TOGETHER
The Joy of Mutual Encouragement!

Ever notice how friendship can fuel your personal growth like you've just been strapped to a rocket? Yeah, that's one of the most powerful parts of having a solid crew. You know that spark of inspiration you get when your friend takes on some wild new adventure or tackles an ambitious goal? That's the charm of collective inspiration fueling everyone's dreams! When we cheer each other on, offer advice, and share experiences, we are like a bunch of motivational speakers buzzing on caffeine and positivity. It's contagious, and before you know it everyone's crushing their goals like it's nothing.

The Domino Effect of Support
Imagine that, your friend mentions they want to start a side hustle, and instead of just giving them a generic "That's cool," you dive in with genuine encouragement—maybe a few tips or links to resources you have come across. Suddenly you have lit a little fire, and before you know it, they are off chasing that dream with renewed energy. And when they succeed, it feels like a victory for you too! It's like one big game of emotional dominoes—one act of support knocks over the next, and suddenly everyone's swept up in the flow of success.

Creating Your Own Growth Squad
Growth isn't a solo mission. Building a *growth squad* is like assembling your own superhero team—but instead of capes, you've got creativity, determination, and maybe an extra shot of espresso. Surround yourself with friends who are just as pumped about their goals as you are, and suddenly you've got a group chat humming with ideas, feedback, and inside jokes. We are talking about creating your own dynamic duos for success—Batman and Robin of personal development, anyone?

Think of your growth squad as a support network that fuels your ambitions. When your friends know your goals, they can help keep you on track. This isn't just about accountability; it's about creating an environment where vulnerability is welcomed and growth is celebrated. They'll be the ones who notice when you seem a little off, gently nudging you back to your path with a supportive word or a shared laugh. Your tribe can see the potential in you that you might overlook during challenging times.

The mutual support fosters a sense of responsibility that drives everyone to strive toward their highest potential. It's like being part of a relay team—each member plays a critical role, and the baton of encouragement is passed seamlessly from one to another. You'll find yourself motivated to take risks and push boundaries, knowing your growth squad is there rooting for you. They're the ones who will remind you that taking a leap of faith is part of the journey, and that each stumble along the way is merely a steppingstone to success.

Voicing your ambitions holds you accountable and also invites your friends to share theirs. This exchange of ideas can spark creativity and innovation, as you collaborate to refine your goals and strategize your next moves. Picture collaborative idea sessions filled with laughter and enthusiasm, where every idea is valued, and every setback is met with resilience and support.

The Power of a Growth Mindset

A growth mindset isn't just about self-help books and inspirational quotes. It's about genuinely believing that we are all capable of improvement and surrounding ourselves with people who reflect that back to us. When we all push each other to grow, it's like being part of a never-ending game of tag—but instead of chasing each other, we are all racing towards success, with the occasional pit stop for celebratory cocktails.

Embracing a growth mindset means recognizing that failure is not a dead end. When one friend misses the mark, the entire squad rallies around them, offering insights and encouragement. This supportive environment transforms setbacks into learning experiences, allowing everyone to build on their strengths and address their weaknesses without fear of judgment.

A growth mindset thrives on curiosity and the willingness to explore. Encourage your friends to share their dreams and aspirations openly, creating a safe space where creativity flourishes. This openness leads to diverse perspectives and sparks ideas that none of you might have considered on your own. A growth mindset is contagious—when one person embraces the idea of growth, it inspires others to do the same.

Mentorship: Your Friendship Secret Weapon

If you really want to take it up a notch, think about creating mentor-mentee pairings in your friend circle. You can team up based on each other's strengths and experiences, creating a dynamic exchange of learning and growth. These relationships are like secret weapons—they give us access to guidance, feedback, and a safe space to grow. You get to teach and learn from each other, creating a powerhouse of growth and good vibes. Plus, nothing says friendship like swapping tips and high-fives (virtual or real).

Fueling Each Other's Fire

I wouldn't have been able to write this book without the constant encouragement from my friend Andrea. I still remember the day I nervously told her about my idea to write it. She didn't just smile and nod; she lit up with excitement and said, "Let's do this!" That small moment sparked a massive wave of support. Andrea didn't just offer encouragement from afar—she became an active partner in the process, stepping in as both a motivator and strategist, guiding me through each step with her energy and insights.

Andrea immediately started brainstorming ways to make the book a reality, coming up with marketing ideas, podcast pitches, and even social media strategies for after the book's launch. She didn't just tell me I could do it, she helped lay out a plan and even put me on a deadline, giving me the push I needed to move from dreaming to doing. I remember bouncing ideas off her, and she would dive right in with feedback, sometimes even more excited than I was. Her fuel kept my fire burning on days when self-doubt crept in.

As we talked about my progress, she shared with me her own goal—shedding the last 20 pounds she had been working on for a while. She looked at me and asked, "Will you support me in this?" Without hesitation, I said, "You bet!" And just like that, our relationship deepened as we encouraged each other on our individual journeys. It was never one-sided. We built each other up every step of the way, finding new ways to help one another stay motivated, whether it was a book deadline or a fitness goal.

Andrea didn't just offer surface-level motivation. Her belief in me—and our ability to push each other—turned what could have been a solo mission into a shared victory. This experience reminded me how powerful mutual encouragement can be and how, with the right people in your corner, you can accomplish so much more than you ever thought possible.

Igniting Growth Together

- **Be Specific with Your Encouragement:** Skip the "nice" and "great" and get real! Say, "That idea sounds impressive! Have you heard of [X tool]? It could help you out." Get the inspiration train rolling!

- **Follow Up:** Don't be the friend who vanishes after the first pep talk. Check in later with a "How's it going with that project? Need any help or feedback?" Show them you are their personal constant source of encouragement!

- **Build Your Squad:** Reach out to friends with complementary skills and set up monthly or biweekly check ins where you discuss your goals and support each other's progress. Create a group chat or regular coffee meetups to share wins, challenges, and resources.

- **Appreciate the Little Steps:** Encourage each other to take pride in progress, no matter how small. Even a quick "Way to go!" when a friend reaches a milestone can create a positive and uplifting atmosphere that motivates everyone to keep moving forward.

- **Cultivate a Mindset for Progress:** When your friend is feeling uncertain, remind them of their strengths and see challenges as a way to grow. A phrase like, "This is challenging, but you're well-equipped to get through it," can offer meaningful support.

- **Gamify Growth & Set Mini Challenges with Friends:** Whoever learns a new skill or reaches a goal first gets treated to a spa day or a virtual happy hour. Turning growth into a game keeps things fun and motivating!

In this vibrant garden of mutual encouragement, every shared experience, every word of support, and every moment of vulnerability becomes a building block for lasting connections, transforming not only our goals but also who we are as individuals. When we lean on each other, we elevate not only our own aspirations but we can also inspire our friends to reach new heights. This interconnectedness amplifies motivation; the excitement of one person's triumph can spark the enthusiasm of another, creating a cascading effect that boosts the entire group.

Together, let's continue pursuing our dreams, knowing that each step taken is an individual victory and a shared journey. The friendships you nurture today will serve as the roots that support your growth tomorrow, turning aspirations into reality.

13
DARE TO BE REAL
The Power of Vulnerability and Authenticity

Imagine for a moment you're with friends, and the conversation takes a turn toward your wildest dreams, secret fears, or goals that seem just out of reach. It's that kind of conversation that starts with laughter and soon dips into deeper waters. You are not merely observing from a distance, you are showing up fully, in all your messy, unfiltered glory. Now, before you run off thinking, "Vulnerability? Hard pass!" stick with me. It's not about sobbing in the cereal aisle (although, no judgment if you do). When you let your guard down and reveal the real you, it sends a message: "I trust you enough to show up as I am." Now you have created a space for real connection—a deep, meaningful bond that goes beyond the surface-level "How's the weather?" chat.

How about, instead of just gossiping about the latest reality show, you dive into what's really weighing on your friend's mind. Suddenly, the conversation gets deep. You realize, *Hey, this is what real friendship feels like!* Vulnerability builds trust, and trust is what makes the friendship glue stick. (You know the strong kind of glue stick—not the cheap stuff that falls apart after a week.)

Vulnerability: The Tightrope That Connects Us

Being vulnerable can feel like walking a tightrope over a pit of awkwardness, and here's the kicker—it's not just about you. When you open up, you give your friends permission to do the same. Think of it like an emotional trust fall. You are both stepping off the edge, but when you land, you are a lot closer than before (and hopefully not covered in bruises).

It's about sharing our triumphs and also exposing our doubts and struggles. This kind of honesty invites deeper conversations which often lead to profound connections. When you bravely share a part of yourself, it encourages your friends to peel back their own layers. Suddenly, you're not just swapping surface-level pleasantries; you're delving into what truly matters.

As you share the real you, you create a space for your friends to empathize with your experiences. This shared understanding can be incredibly healing for everyone involved. The more you reveal your authentic self, the more your friends feel they can do the same. You realize that you're not alone in your feelings, and it's in these moments of openness that genuine transformation unfolds—as individuals, and as a community.

Embrace Authenticity

In a world full of filters and carefully curated Instagram lives, being authentically you is like discovering a hidden treasure. No map needed. When you own your quirks and weirdness, you not only feel freer, but you also inspire your friends to drop their masks and do the same. Authenticity is the ingredient that turns ordinary conversations into unforgettable connections.

When you let your true self shine, you create an atmosphere where friends feel safe to drop their pretenses. Picture this: At a gathering, someone brings up that embarrassing story from high school about wearing two different shoes to prom. Instead of cringing, you share your own mortifying moment—like the time you tripped on stage during a school play while trying to impress that cute classmate. Laughter fills the room as everyone recalls their own epic fails, creating a night of lighthearted camaraderie.

As the laughter settles, something shifts. That simple story unlocks a deep layer of connection. With the tension of perfection lifted, you feel empowered to share more about the lingering embarrassment of that stumble, how it made you hesitant to take risks in the future, and how vulnerability often feels like a precarious path. Your friends, inspired by your honesty, share their own stories of failure and the fears that haunt them, revealing a shared humanity that transcends the surface chatter.

In that moment, you realize that authenticity isn't just about sharing laughs; it's about creating a space where true feelings can flow. By embracing your imperfections, you strengthen your bond with your friends and foster an environment where profound dialogue can thrive. Together, you explore the complexities of vulnerability, transforming a night of shared humor into a profound experience of mutual support and understanding.

A Simple Text, A Lifeline: Finding Strength in Vulnerability

When I lost my job after my company was acquired, it wasn't just about losing a paycheck—it felt like the ground beneath me shifted in a way I hadn't expected. After more than 25 years in corporate America, I found myself without a daily routine and an income, while also juggling stress at home with my kids and personal life. I felt unsettled and unsure about how to move forward.

I definitely felt stuck—unsure of how to talk about what I was going through or who I could turn to. There was a fear of not wanting to burden my friends, especially since everyone seemed to have their own things going on. I let that fear keep me quiet longer than I probably should have, but deep down I was just afraid of what would happen next and how to regain control over the parts of my life that felt like they were slipping.

Sometimes, the smallest acts can change everything. Two friends reached out when I least expected it and exactly when I needed it. One of them sent me a simple text: "I know things have been heavy—how about lunch? My treat." It wasn't just the offer of a meal; it was the invitation to talk and be heard. The other friend said, "Call me anytime, day or night. I'm here for you." These were small gestures, but they opened the door for me to be vulnerable, to finally talk about what I was going through.

That lunch and that phone call turned into safe spaces where I could share openly. I didn't feel judged or like I was burdening anyone. My friends listened patiently, allowing me to express all my concerns and fears. Through those vulnerable conversations, our bond grew stronger, transforming the moment from simply unloading my emotions into a shared experience where they could reveal their struggles too. Those simple acts of support were a turning point, reminding me that even in uncertain times, I wasn't alone and that I had a solid circle of people I could lean on.

Vulnerability doesn't have to involve a deep philosophical conversation—it's being brave enough to share a little piece of your heart and realizing that your friends are there to catch you when you stumble. Those moments of connection became my lifeline during that tough time, and it all started with two simple texts that led to conversations that changed everything.

Making Room for the Real Stuff

- **Start Small, Build Gradually:** You don't need to dive into the deep end of your emotions right away. Test the waters with a small, meaningful share, like "Honestly, work's been stressing me out lately." Think of it as dipping your toes into the vulnerability pool before doing a cannonball—and ask for vulnerability in return by saying, "How are things on your end?" It creates balance in conversation.

- **Create a Safe Space for Others:** Let your friends know they can share with you, no strings attached. Say something like, "I'm here for whatever you need, no judgments." It's like building a cozy clubhouse where secrets and laughs are welcome, and we can kick back without putting up a front. When they do open up, reassure them by saying, "I really appreciate you sharing that with me—it means a lot." This gives your friend a green light to be 100% themselves.

- **Embrace & Encourage Realness:** Own your quirks, whether it's your obsession with rewatching Twilight or your weird love for collecting random knick-knacks, let it shine, and encourage your friends to do the same. There is nothing more vulnerable than saying, "Yeah, I have an entire shelf dedicated to tiny plants, and I'm not sorry about it." After a deep conversation, reassure your friend. "I love how real you are with me—it's refreshing." It's like giving them a fist bump for being brave.

- **Check in & Be Patient:** Vulnerability isn't a one-time deal—it's a long game. Keep the connection strong by regularly checking in, "How's that thing we talked about going?" Be patient if they're not ready to spill everything right away. Let them know you're always ready to listen whenever they're ready to talk. It's about creating trust, not rushing them to share their life story. (Unless they want to, then by all means, grab some popcorn.)

As you step onto that tightrope, it will feel scary at first, and each leap of faith brings you closer to your friends and encourages them to join you in embracing their own vulnerabilities. Together, you can foster a circle of trust filled with growth and meaningful connections. So take a deep breath and embrace the wobble!

14

FROM HURT TO HEALING
The Art of Apologies and Letting Go

Even with strong bonds, slip-ups are inevitable, because, well, we're human. Sometimes it's as simple as forgetting to text back, and other times it's a little more serious, like the time you accidentally drank the last glass of that special wine. Whoopsie! These blunders can be lighthearted or significant, and still what truly matters is how we respond. Forgiving and apologizing isn't just about smoothing things over—it's an opportunity to strengthen our relationships, even when wine is on the line.

Owning Your Mistakes: The Art of Apologizing

Apologizing can feel like trying to fit a square peg in a round hole—uncomfortable and sometimes just plain hard to pull off. But it's worth it. A good apology isn't just about tossing out a *sorry* like you're handing out Halloween candy. Nope, it's about owning your own blunders and showing you really get why your friend's feelings are valid. Bonus points if you can follow up with action that says, "I'm committed to not making that mistake again (no more midnight wine thief)."

When you apologize sincerely, it opens the door for healing and shows the other person that their feelings matter. It's not about being perfect; it's about being accountable.

Embrace Empathy

Empathy is the bridge that keeps this whole apologizing-and-forgiving process connected. Whether you're the one saying sorry or the one trying to let go, empathy allows you to see things from your friend's perspective. Think of it as swapping shoes for a day—you just might discover how those blisters feel!

Be sure to understand the full story first—trying to empathize without context is like squeezing into a pair of 6 inch heels: uncomfortable and bound to cause trouble. For example, if your friend seems upset after a casual comment, take a moment to reflect on what might have triggered their reaction. Maybe it's not just about that offhand remark; perhaps they're dealing with something deeper.

When you invest the time to see things from your friend's perspective, you not only honor their emotions, you also cultivate a space where open conversations can unfold.

Letting Go: The Freedom in Forgiveness

Forgiveness can feel a bit like letting go of that one sock that's been stuck in your drawer for months. It's hard to part ways, but once you do, there's relief. Holding onto grudges can weigh you down emotionally, taking up space that could be filled with positive energy. Forgiving someone doesn't mean you're giving them a free pass to repeat mistakes—it's about freeing yourself from that emotional baggage, creating room for healing and moving forward. It's a way of saying, "I value our relationship more than holding onto this grudge."

Communication Opens the Door

When it comes to mending friendships, communication is like the front-door key—keeping things open and accessible. Whether you're offering an apology or working through forgiveness, it's about talking things out in a way that says, "Let's understand each other" rather than "Here's why you were wrong." Real communication invites both sides to share openly, creating an atmosphere where empathy and understanding can thrive. A meaningful exchange allows space for each person's perspective to be heard, helping to avoid misunderstandings and build a foundation for a stronger connection moving forward.

Moving Forward Together (Because Going It Alone Is Overrated)

Once you have done the heavy lifting of apologizing and forgiving, it's time to walk the walk—together. The next chapter of your friendship might be a little different, but it can be better, stronger, and more in sync.

Forgiveness Is for You, Too

Don't forget to give yourself a little grace along the way. We all mess up—even when we are trying our best. Forgiving yourself is like turning the page to a fresh chapter in your mental book. Take what you have learned, move forward, and don't let the guilt linger.

A Long-Awaited Apology: Healing After Hurt

One of my new Arizona pals, Whitney, shared with me a story that captures the power of forgiveness. She had a childhood friend she had known since middle school—they were inseparable, sharing everything from clothes to awkward phases, and thanks to Whitney, she met the man who would later become her husband. They were more like sisters than friends, navigating life's highs and lows side by side. But after her friend got married, things started to shift. At first, the changes were subtle, almost unnoticeable, but over time, a particular behavior began to drive a wedge between them.

Whenever Whitney and her friend were out together, her friend had developed a habit of correcting Whitney's English mid-conversation. It was small at first—correcting a word here and there or offering an alternative phrase. But as time went on, it became more frequent and public. It wasn't just the corrections; it was the way they made Whitney feel—embarrassed and belittled, especially when it happened in front of others. The dynamic, once lighthearted and fun, now felt uncomfortable and strained.

One evening, after yet another public correction that left Whitney feeling humiliated, she decided to speak up. She approached her friend in private and explained how the constant *fixing* of her language was making her feel small. But her friend didn't take it well. Instead of apologizing, she became defensive, brushing it off as no big deal and insisting that Whitney was overreacting. Hurt and frustrated, Whitney began to pull away. She didn't want to lose her friend, but she also couldn't keep subjecting herself to the constant corrections and the feelings of inadequacy they stirred up.

As the months passed, their once-close friendship turned into occasional, surface-level interactions. Eventually, they stopped talking altogether. Years went by, and though Whitney had moved on, the unresolved tension always lingered in the back of her mind. Then, out of nowhere, Whitney's phone rang, and it was her friend. The apology that followed was long overdue. Her friend explained that she hadn't realized at the time how her behavior had hurt Whitney. She admitted that she had been defensive when Whitney first brought it up, but with the passage of time, she had gained perspective. Now, she wanted to make things right.

The apology wasn't just words—it was filled with genuine remorse. Whitney could hear the sincerity in her friend's voice, and something inside her softened. After all these years, her friend had reflected on her actions and reached out with a heartfelt apology. It was the closure Whitney hadn't realized she needed. Forgiveness didn't happen instantly, but it opened the door for healing.

In friendships, mistakes happen, and people often don't realize the impact of their actions in the moment. True healing comes from owning those mistakes and offering a sincere apology, even if it takes years. Forgiveness, on the other hand, is about letting go of the hurt—to free yourself, not just to benefit the other person. Remember, friendships aren't about avoiding mistakes—they're about how we handle them when they happen, and the strength that comes from navigating those challenges together.

Essential Strategies for Relationship Repair

- **How to Apologize Like You Mean It**
    - **Acknowledge the Impact:** Be specific about what happened and how your actions affected them. For example, say, "I know I hurt you when I didn't show up when you needed me." Specificity shows you understand the impact of your actions.
    - **Ask How They Feel:** When offering an apology, ask your friend how they felt about the situation. "Will you tell me how this affected you?" This shows you care about their perspective and creates space for empathy.
    - **Owning Up & Following Through on them:** Throw in some real feels, "I realize that probably made you feel unimportant, and I'm really sorry." It's about validation, not just saying the words. Apologies are like rain checks—you've got to follow through on them. Next time, show you have learned by saying something like, "Next movie night, drinks are on me, and I promise not to ghost you." Your actions will reinforce your words and show that you are committed to improvement.

- **When You're the One Who's Hurt: Expressing Your Feelings**
    - **Use "I" Statements:** Instead of launching into "You hurt me when..." try something softer, like, "I felt hurt when..."

It's less accusatory and more about how you feel.

- **Offer Understanding:** "I get it, we all mess up, and I want to move past this with you." It's less about being perfect and more about understanding that we are all human and make mistakes.

- Turning the Page: Moving Forward Together
    - **Reflect on Your Emotions & Let Them Go for Yourself:** Before forgiving, take a hot minute to really understand how you feel. Once you've got that clarity, letting go of resentment becomes easier. Let go for *you*, not just them. Try an affirmation like, "I'm letting this go so I can sleep better at night" (and stop thinking about that wine incident). Write down what you have learned from a past mistake and remind yourself that growth is a process, not a race. Then mentally let go of the guilt.

    - **Decide What's Next:** Forgiveness can be a magical factory reset button. Define what moving forward looks like—whether it's a fresh start or a new set of boundaries, make a plan. It could be as simple as, "Next time, let's both try to communicate better." Boom—instant teamwork. After a week or so, check in with the other person. Say, "How are you feeling about our conversation?" It shows that you are still invested in keeping things strong.

    - **Set Personal Growth Goals:** Use those slip-ups to fuel your future self. Set small goals like "Next time, I'll be more mindful of how I react."

In the end, apologizing and forgiving isn't about keeping score—it's about nurturing friendships that are healthy, strong, and refreshingly human. After all, life's too short to carry around grudges (or wine-related guilt). Embrace the messiness, learn from the missteps, and cherish the connections that allow you to grow together. Letting go of resentment paves the way for laughter and deeper understanding, making each shared moment a little brighter.

15

FRIENDSHIP GRATITUDE GOALS
Reflect, Love, and Live with a Thankful Heart!

While forgiveness helps clear the air, gratitude keeps friendships shining. After all, friendships are like gold, only better because you can't call gold at 3am to vent about life! At the heart of every strong friendship is the power of gratitude—nothing says *you matter to me* quite like taking a moment to actually *say it*. Sure, we like to believe our friends already know how much they mean to us, but even the best of friends need to hear it now and then. And why keep all that love bottled up when you can shower them with it instead?

Gratitude doesn't mean you need to break out into a tear-filled monologue (unless that's your thing). Sometimes, it's the simplest, most unexpected gestures that pack the biggest punch. A quick "Thank you for always being down for sushi" or "You're the best thing since morning coffee" can totally make their day—and let's be honest, who doesn't want to be someone's personal caffeine boost?

Embrace the Power of "I Appreciate You"
We're not talking larger than life, swoon-worthy gestures. It's more about casually dropping those mini thank-yous like, "Hey, thanks for always listening to my rants about that obscure hobby I picked up during quarantine" or "I'm so glad to have you in my life." These tiny tokens of gratitude seem subtle; trust me, they hit harder than a double shot of espresso.

Think about weaving gratitude into the everyday—like a little extra sparkle in the routine. And don't hold back, tell your friends how much they mean to you. Show them you appreciate their kooky humor, their endless support, and yes, even their questionable taste in movies. Gratitude brings positivity and happiness, not just to those you love, but to yourself as well. When it comes down to it, friendship is all about showing up, loving hard, and making sure your people know they are the champions in your life.

Don't Be Afraid to Say "I Love You"
Why is it that we can easily tell our coffee, *I love you* (because, let's face it,

it deserves it), but saying it to a friend feels like jumping out of a plane? Guess what? Telling your friends *I love you* is just as necessary—and less terrifying than skydiving. Friend love is real love, people! When you drop those three little words, you are basically handing them a gold-star sticker for being marvelous.

The Simple Hug of Gratitude

My aunt shared a beautiful story with me about the power of small acts of love and the gratitude they create. In one week, two of her close friends were hit with major health battles. Julia had just come home from back surgery, dealing with intense pain that nothing seemed to ease. Meanwhile, Doria had been diagnosed with Parkinson's disease, and the weight of the news was overwhelming. My aunt was heartbroken for them both, wondering how she could possibly help.

When words and advice felt inadequate, she leaned on the simplest form of care she knew—showing up. She called each friend and said, "Dinner will be at your house at 6pm tonight." It wasn't about the food itself—just a basic lasagna, salad, and bread—but it was the gesture, the reminder that they weren't alone. And for her friends, it meant the world.

Julia and Doria, along with their husbands, expressed their gratitude over and over, not just for the meal, but for the friendship. They told my aunt how her thoughtfulness and presence helped lift their spirits during a dark time. The focus wasn't on solving their problems, but on making them feel seen and cared for. My aunt's small act became a source of comfort, and the appreciation her friends expressed deepened their bonds even further.

This story is a beautiful reminder that sometimes, showing gratitude means simply showing up—and those moments, in turn, spark deep appreciation and love in others. Gratitude has a way of spreading far beyond the initial act, and my aunt's friends made sure she knew how much her kindness had touched them. They expressed their heartfelt thanks repeatedly, not only for the meal but for the genuine care and friendship that accompanied it. Their gratitude was a clear reminder that even the simplest gestures can resonate deeply, transforming moments of hardship into moments of connection and care.

Thankful Heart Habits

- **Start a Gratitude Journal:** Each week, jot down one thing you appreciate about your closest friends—maybe their impeccable taste in music or the fact they always answer your texts within 0.4 seconds. And when the mood strikes, share the gratitude with them. (Trust me, it'll make their day.)

- **Send "Appreciation" Texts:** On a random Tuesday, shoot your friend a text saying, "I was thinking about you today and just wanted to say I really appreciate you." It takes two seconds, and it might just turn their entire day around.

- **Daily Gratitude Check In:** Before you start or end your day, think of one friend who positively affected you that day—maybe it was the one who sent you that perfectly timed *You got this* GIF. Give them a shoutout, even if it's just, "Hey, thanks for being spectacular today."

- **Create an Appreciation Ritual:** Set aside a time weekly or monthly to reflect on your friendships. Light a candle or go for a walk while thinking about all the ways your friends contribute to your happiness and well-being. This mindfulness practice will reinforce your sense of gratitude for the people in your life.

Life becomes so much richer when you take a moment to appreciate the amazing people around you—the ones who leave you in stitches or jump to the rescue for even the smallest fashion emergency. The more gratitude you express, the clearer it becomes how fortunate you are to have such wonderful souls in your life. When you acknowledge these special connections, you don't just enrich your friendships—you nurture a deeper sense of contentment and happiness in yourself.

16

FRIENDS ARE LIKE A PUZZLE
Each One Brings a Different Piece

Alright, so we just talked about gratitude, and now it's time to focus on *who* you're grateful for—and what each friend uniquely brings to your life! Take note here: No one friend, family member, or partner is going to be your one-stop-shop for everything. That's why we have a *whole squad* of friends! Each one brings their own flavor to the mix, like the one-of-a-kind toppings on a sundae—some are sweet, some are surprising, but together they make the whole thing way better. One friend might be your go-to for deep, soul-baring conversations, while another is your spontaneous, "Let's book a trip tomorrow!" adventure buddy. The key is recognizing what each person brings to the table—because honestly, the table would be pretty dull without their contributions.

Think of it this way—your friends are like a puzzle, and each one has that special piece that makes your life picture complete. Some friends are the corner pieces that hold things steady, and others are those weird-shaped ones that don't fit anywhere else and somehow make the picture come alive.

Knowing which friend to reach out to for specific things isn't just smart—it's friendship gold. Instead of leaning on one person for every crisis, laugh, or late-night chat, spread the love across your circle. Not only does this avoid overwhelming any one friend, but it also makes everyone feel valued for what they uniquely bring to your life. Think of it like tapping into a friend's unique talents when you need them most—one friend might be your pep talk expert, while another is a master at planning spontaneous adventures. Letting friends shine in their own way keeps your connections balanced and makes each friend feel truly appreciated. It's like giving them all a chance to flex their friendship A-game!

Having a range of friends is like having a toolbox full of different gadgets—each one does something special. You've got the friend who's basically your life coach, the one who reminds you it's okay to eat cake for breakfast, and the one who somehow knows all the random trivia. Let them shine in their own roles! Appreciate each one for what they uniquely bring, instead of wishing they could all be everything rolled into one.

Piecing Together Support: Letting Each Friend Shine

When I began writing this book, I was fueled by passion and quickly realized that not every friend could handle the constant updates about my progress or the endless asks for feedback. This lesson hit home for me. It became clear that while my friends were supportive, I needed to be mindful of how I reached out for help, ensuring I didn't exhaust any one person with my writing process.

That's when I embraced the idea that each friend brings a different piece to the puzzle. I looked across my amazing tribe and realized I didn't need one person to support me through everything. For creative design, I leaned on my visually artistic friend. For humor, I knew exactly who to call for a sprinkle of wit in my writing. And when it came time for the final edit before handing it to a professional, I turned to my Auntie, whose detail-oriented approach was exactly what I needed.

My tribe became my fuel in this process. Sometimes all I needed was a simple "Keep Going," and I knew exactly which friend to text for that boost of motivation. By spreading out the requests for help and tailoring them to each friend's strengths, I was able to keep my support system strong, engaged, and excited for me, rather than overwhelmed by constant asks. In the end, I didn't just produce a book—I created a collaborative work, with each friend contributing something unique to the final product. Together, they helped me pull together something pretty special, and I didn't burn anyone out in the process.

Each person in my circle added their own flare, and it reminded me that no single friend needs to carry the entire weight of my dreams or challenges. We each have our strengths, and when combined they complete the puzzle and everything fits together beautifully.

Your Friendship Game Plan

- **Create a Friendship Strength Map:** Make a list of your closest friends and jot down their distinct qualities or strengths. Who's your go-to for advice? Who always knows how to turn your mood around with a joke? This will help you be intentional about who you lean on and for what.

- **Call on Their Strengths:** When you need advice or support, think about each friend's strengths. Feeling stuck? Try going to your creative friend for fresh ideas. Need some hard truths? Reach out to the one friend who's refreshingly blunt (maybe take it with a grain of salt). Choosing the right friend for the moment keeps things balanced, helps you avoid leaning on the same person, and strengthens your connections all around.

- **Mix Up Your Support Network:** Instead of always going to the same person for every vent session or pep talk, rotate who you turn to based on what's happening. Not only does this keep you from overwhelming one friend, but it also fortifies friendships with everyone in your circle by letting each person show up in the ways they're best at.

- **Practice Gratitude for Each Friend's Role:** Yup, back to the gratitude! Once a week, send a quick message to a different friend thanking them for what they bring to your life. Something like, "I really appreciate how you always know how to make me laugh when I need it most." Trust me, it'll make their day.

Embrace it—your friends are all unique for a reason! They bring variety, balance, and a whole lot of spice to your life. Let each friend shine in their own way, appreciating the role they play in your bigger picture. The more you lean into their strengths, the more epic your collective friendship puzzle becomes!

FROM MEMES TO MEMORIES
🦩🦩🦩 The Fun Side of Friendship

Friendship is one of life's greatest adventures, and what better way to celebrate that than by having a blast together? Friends bring a unique flavor to our lives, and this next bit is all about the fun we create—whether it's through shared memes, spontaneous dance parties, or those inside jokes that bring tears of joy.

It's time to dive into the fun side of friendship. We are going to take a moment to think about how technology helps us stay connected and keep those bonds strong, even amidst the chaos of daily life. I see my kids out there staying in touch with nearly thousands of people, and while we're just talking about our inner circle, I've come to realize how technology has opened up a world of possibilities for staying close to the people who matter most. Whether it's hosting a virtual game night or sending a playlist that feels like a hug from afar, technology—and the global pandemic—has revolutionized our ways of staying close, with no turning back.

I want to laugh every day. Don't you? Some inside jokes between my friends and me still have me laughing until I cry, even years later. Music too—oh, I have so many songs that are *my song* (my little tribe is laughing as they read this). My bestie in Seattle just shared with me an awesome playlist "Confidence Boost" and it got us both up and going last week. It was this awesome way for us to stay connected even though we're miles apart. I'll be honest—being alone in a new state hasn't been easy, but when a friend says, "Let's watch this show together," it feels like I'm right there with them. However, true crime is a firm NO—I refuse to watch it because I get too scared being home alone!

Celebrating each other is just as crucial as laughter, so let's channel our inner cheerleaders and give our friends a serious pep rally! Whether you're shouting out milestones, throwing epic surprise parties, or shooting a quick text that says "You're absolutely killing it!" these little acts are like a burst of sunshine for the soul. They remind us that we're in this voyage together!

When we take the time to celebrate every win, big or small, we're not just reinforcing our friendships; we're cranking up the joy dial in our lives. Make it a habit to pop the metaphorical champagne for each other, dance like nobody's watching, and create a culture of positivity that makes every moment feel like a celebration!

What about traditions? Are they just for families to create? NOPE! I have one friend who's the queen of creating traditions—she's always planning something fun, from Halloween progressive parties, *favorite things* gift soirees to holiday cookie exchanges. And while everyone knows I don't bake, I still love coming up with something creative to bring. These traditions, whether they're in person or virtual, help create memories and strengthen bonds.

Staying in touch is oh so important and so is being intentional with how we use tools, moments and creativity to bring joy, laughter, and connection into our lives. So get ready because this section is jam-packed with actionable creative ideas to help make your friendships more meaningful and a whole lot of fun!

17
BEYOND THE LOLS
Use Tech with a Flair!

Sure, it's easy to send a meme or react to your friend's story, but come on—we can do better! Technology is a splendid way to keep friendships thriving, but why stop at a lazy LOL? Add a dash of personality and thoughtfulness! Instead of just dropping that meme into the chat, tell them *why* it reminded you of the time they slipped on ice while trying to look cool. Trust me, that little extra flair makes all the difference—like adding glitter to a birthday card. Sure, it's messy, but it's memorable!

Virtual Hangouts—The New Social Scene
Gone are the days of *only* meeting at a coffee shop for catchups (thanks, global chaos!). We have the internet superhighway, and it's a goldmine of ways to hang out without needing pants. Virtual movie nights, Zoom happy hours, or even synchronized snack breaks—get creative! Syncing a movie and texting your thoughts like you're Siskel & Ebert? Now *that's* quality time.

Netflix & Bonding
You know what's better than watching Netflix alone? Watching it at the same time as your bestie and sending real-time reaction GIFs. Instead of just texting, "You need to watch this," link up and turn it into a full-on event. Grab the gummy bears, hit play, and let the binge-watching begin. Whether you're both sobbing at a rom-com or yelling at the screen because the main character made the dumbest decision ever, it's a shared experience from wherever you're lounging, snacks in hand.

Play Together Online
Games aren't just for kids or your cousin's Fortnite addiction. Bring out the competitive spirit by playing online games together. Whether it's a savage round of Mario Kart Tour or a surprisingly intense session of digital Pictionary, you'll bond over victories and laugh at each other's virtual misfortunes. Major props for trash talk delivered with love.

Snail Mail Meets Digital World
Snail mail is cute and all, but let's be honest—it's the 21st century, and

we have so many options. Take your creativity to the next level with digital postcards or surprise video messages. It's like sending a love letter, but with less risk of it being lost under a sea of catalogs and flyers.

Share Your Day in a Fun Way

Sure, you could send a regular old text to update your friend about your day, but why not kick it up a notch? SnapChat or Marco Polo lets you share video snippets of your day without feeling the pressure of live calls. Plus, you get the fun of sending ridiculous faces or live updates like, "Look at me folding laundry for the third time this week. Thrilling, I know."

Virtual Book Club

A virtual book club? Yes, please! Imagine cozying up in your PJs with a great book and your favorite beverage—whether it's a fancy cocktail, a comforting cup of tea, or that bottle of wine you've been saving. No need for uncomfortable silences or small talk; just dive into engaging stories that spark lively discussions!

You can keep it classy with literary masterpieces or go for a guilty pleasure with a delightfully trashy novel. Who doesn't love dissecting the plot of a ridiculous romance or debating the motivations of an over-the-top villain? And the best part? You don't have to leave your couch! Grab that drink, mute your mic when you need to, and join in on the fun from the comfort of your own home.

Plus, you can rotate who picks the book each month, ensuring a delightful mix of genres and styles. Whether you're reading the latest bestseller or rediscovering a childhood favorite, every meeting is a chance to bond, laugh, and share insights. Gather your friends, set a date, and get ready for some unforgettable literary adventures!

Surprise Digital Deliveries

Feeling generous? Send your friend a surprise delivery like their favorite lunch via UberEats or an e-gift card for coffee. Who doesn't love a surprise treat showing up out of nowhere, just because? It's like digital magic—only instead of pulling a rabbit out of a hat, you're delivering tacos straight to their door.

Keep the Group Chats Alive

We all have that one dead group chat that fizzled out after the excitement of organizing a group trip. Revive it! Drop in a ridiculous GIF, share a random thought, or challenge the group to send the funniest comedy clip of the week. Group chats don't have to be functional—they can be your daily dose of chaos and giggles.

Press Play: Staying Connected, One Netflix Show at a Time

One of my favorite memories during the pandemic (yes, there were a few silver linings) was watching a reality show on Netflix with my bestie. Even though we were stuck at our own homes, we were determined to keep up our 'virtual hangouts'. Now neither of us could figure out how to use the fancy apps that were supposed to sync our screens, so we came up with our own low-tech solution: We'd hop on a phone call, count down from three, and press play at the exact same time.

What followed were hours of pure entertainment, watching our favorite show in unison over the phone. We'd pause at the juiciest moments to analyze the drama, share our thoughts, and laugh until we cried. Every week, we'd look forward to the night when new episodes dropped, making it our ritual when we couldn't be together in person. Even though we weren't physically sitting on the same couch, we were still sharing the same moments and inside jokes, just like old times.

Those Netflix nights became more than just a distraction from the chaos outside—they were our way of staying connected and keeping our friendship strong when everything else felt uncertain. It was proof that even when life throws you a detour, a little creativity and technology can keep the laughter and connection alive.

Virtual Friendship Hacks

- **Turn Screen Time into Memory Time:** Treat virtual hangouts like exclusive events—whether it's syncing up for a Netflix show using Teleparty (which no, I never did figure out) and giving live commentary or sharing a casual breakfast over video chat in your pajamas. It's all about turning everyday moments into special ones, even if it's just cereal on a Thursday morning.

- **Game On, Virtually:** Challenge each other with multiplayer apps like Houseparty for game nights where you can roast each other in real time. For a competitive twist, set up trivia challenges and see who reigns supreme—Heads up. It's the one who cheats by Googling answers.

- **Get Creative with Digital Connections:** Don't limit yourself to texts—send thoughtful video messages when you want to reach out but don't feel like a full FaceTime session. Apps like *Canva* and *Touchnote* allow you to send quirky digital postcards, it's modern, fast, and your friend won't have to pretend they didn't see the postcard hiding under that pile of Amazon packages!

- **Kick Off Fun Streaks:** Begin a SnapStreak where you send silly selfies daily (double chin mandatory) or set weekly themes like "Meme Monday" or "Throwback Thursday" to keep your group chat buzzing with funny content and inside jokes.

- **Join the Virtual Book & Media Club:** Host a virtual book chat, just pick a book, grab your beverage of choice, and gossip over Zoom like you're at an actual café (minus the overpriced pastries) or bonus points for themed snacks or cocktails that match the book's setting. Reading a novel set in Italy? You *must* have wine. Or sync up shows and send each other real-time reactions via text—because every Netflix docudrama deserves some commentary.

- **Surprise & Delight:** Brighten your friend's week with a surprise digital subscription box, like a one-time delivery of a meditation app, a digital magazine they love, or even an audiobook credit. Or maybe they need a caffeine boost so send over an e-gift card for their favorite coffee shop with a note "I can't be there, but coffee is on me!" It's the next best thing to teleportation.

Remember, technology isn't just a handy tool—it's your creativity amplifier! So, ditch the ordinary social shares and texts, and unleash your imagination to transform friendships into extraordinary adventures! Let your digital interactions become unforgettable moments that spark joy and connection, turning the everyday into something truly sensational!

18
PODCASTS, PLAYLISTS, AND CHILL
Friendships at Play

Of course, no amount of technology can replace one key ingredient in friendships—laughter. It's like guacamole on a taco—everything's better with that extra zing! Beyond the humor, it's the shared experiences that make all the difference, whether you're swapping playlists, discovering new podcasts, or diving into binge-worthy shows together. These shared moments kickstart conversations and laughter that pull us out of the everyday routine and bring something fresh to the friendship. Whether it's laughing until you're out of breath because someone tripped over their own feet (you know who you are), or bonding over a song that gets stuck in your head for days, these moments give friendships a playful shake-up and bring fresh energy when life starts to feel a bit too familiar.

You're not just laughing together; you're crafting inside jokes and memorable moments that add spice to your friendship. So pull up a chair (and maybe some popcorn) because we're jumping into all the ways friendships make life richer, brighter, and infinitely more entertaining!

Laughter: The Ultimate Bonding Tool
Laughter is more than just a mood booster—it's the spark that ignites connections and keeps friendships vibrant, real, and resilient. When you're laughing with friends, walls come down, insecurities take a back seat, and even the toughest days feel a little lighter. It's those awesome moments when everything else fades, and you're just two people reveling in the pure joy of a shared and often ridiculous experience. Whether it's cracking up over inside jokes, making goofy faces during a video call, or recalling that time you tried to host a fancy dinner party and ended up with burnt pizza and wine from a box, laughter builds trust and fosters a sense of belonging.

It's also a reset button—laughter can turn a bad mood into a good one in seconds, reminding us not to take life too seriously. Those moments when you're laughing so hard you feel like you might burst are the snapshots of life that stay with you, creating memories that bring you back to each other time and time again. Embrace those giggles, snorts, and side-splitting laughs—every chuckle is a building block in the house of friendship.

Sharing Music: The Soundtrack of Your Friendship

Remember that time you heard a song and thought, "This is SO [insert friend's name]?" That's because music is basically a time machine wrapped in a catchy tune. When you share your favorite tracks or send a song that reminds you of your friend, it's giving them a little piece of your soul, or at least your Spotify playlist.

Whether it's a jam that you can't stop blasting or a song that gives you all the feels, sharing music connects you in ways words can't. It's your way of saying, "I know you'll vibe with this," and the shared experience often leads to hilarious dance-offs, sing-alongs, or just a good laugh at the lyrics.

Podcasts: The New "Let's Grab Coffee"

Podcasts are those great conversation starters that never run out of steam. Whether you're into murder mysteries or shows that teach you how to adult, sharing your latest obsessions keeps you and your friends connected in a whole new way. It's as though you're in the same book club—without the pressure of actually reading anything. Plus, you can analyze every episode like it's a college essay (but way more fun), often leading to laugh-out-loud moments as you recount the wildest stories or the most absurd takes. Suddenly, you've got hours of conversation material and plenty of inside jokes to keep the laughter rolling—true crime junkies unite!

Catchphrase Bingo: Where Laughs & Prizes Await

Inside jokes are one of the best parts of close friendships, so why not turn them into a game with *Inside Joke Bingo?* Here's how it works: Each friend fills out a bingo card with classic catchphrases, funny habits, or signature moves that you and your group are known for. Maybe your friend Jenn always quotes *Schitt's Creek*, or Dave never fails to spill something on his shirt at every dinner. As you go through your days together, mark off each inside joke or classic quirk as it happens.

This game is a fantastic way to appreciate the little, familiar things about each other that make your friendship special. It's also guaranteed laughter each time one of these 'bingo-worthy' moments happens. And when someone finally shouts, "Bingo!" you'll all be laughing at the thought of how predictably delightful your crew can be. Consider keeping a small prize for the winner—a funny trinket or the honor of picking your next hangout spot.

Bloopers & Boogies: Your TikTok Challenge Awaits
You don't need dance skills to rock a TikTok Dance Challenge; the fun is in the attempt! Pick a popular TikTok dance that's trending (or any silly choreography you find) and try to learn it together. You might surprise yourselves with some actual moves—or end up completely out of sync and cracking up over how bad you are. Either way, it's an activity that brings you close, gets you moving, and fills your phone with funny outtakes you can look back on later.

To add a little extra fun, take turns judging each other's versions, or vote for "most improved" at the end. If you're really bold, you can post it online—no need to worry about perfection; everyone will love seeing you two having a blast. Even if you never become TikTok-famous, you'll have the memories (and videos) to look back on.

Turning Miles into Moments with Podcasts
When Andrea and I packed up and left Seattle, we both had long, solo drives ahead of us to our new homes—Andrea headed to Texas, and me to Arizona on the exact same day. Andrea is *obsessed* with podcasts—she's always raving about the funniest comedy ones and the most gripping murder mysteries. I'll be honest, on road trips I've always been more of a "blast my music and sing along" kind of girl, but Andrea was insistent. She told me, "You *have* to try these podcasts for your drive, trust me!" I hesitated at first because podcasts have never been my go-to. But Andrea was so excited about it, so I decided to give it a shot.

And guess what? I got hooked! Before I knew it, I was laughing out loud in the car and getting way too invested in a whodunit story. It was as if Andrea was right there with me sharing in the experience. Even though she's in Texas and I'm here in Arizona, we've found this new way to stay connected. We text each other about the latest episodes, send voice notes reacting to the plot twists, and it's become this fun little tradition between us.

It's these shared moments, like discovering a love for the same podcasts, that make our long-distance friendship feel close. And yes, we also bond over the very different bug varieties we've both encountered in our new states—scorpions and tarantulas, anyone? Yikes!

The laughter we share over our favorite episodes and the absurdity of our conversations bring us joy and lighten even the heaviest days. After all, whether it's through a catchy podcast theme song or an uproarious plot twist, these moments of laughter form a link of joy through our friendship, keeping us close no matter the distance.

Friendship Entertainment Guide

- **Laughter & Shared Experiences**
    - **Create Inside Jokes & Share Daily Laughs:** Anytime something hilarious happens, lock it in the memory bank. Inside jokes are like the secret handshake of friendship—totally silly, but oh-so-important. Keep the laughs coming by sending a daily dad joke (those are so hilarious), TikTok, or a funny video. Laughter is a daily requirement, and you, my friend, are the supplier.
    - **Add a Twist to Your Hangouts:** Start a round of Inside Joke Bingo or a hilarious TikTok dance challenge! And don't stop there—mix things up with new experiences like an online cooking class one week or a creative project the next! These small, playful activities bring laughter and keep your friendships feeling fresh.

- **Music & Media Bonding**
    - **Shared Playlist & Host a Virtual Listening Fun:** Make a collaborative playlist on Spotify or Apple Music where you can both add songs. Call it "Our Life Soundtrack" or "Bops and Bangers." Queue up that new album, hit play at the same time, and text each other your professional (or not-so-professional) reviews. Whether the chorus slaps or the beat's off, the shared experience is the fun part!
    - **Start a Podcast Club & Swap Recommendations:** Just like a book club, pick a podcast to binge each week, then swap hot takes like, "Can you believe that twist in episode 3?!" You can also share recommendations based on personality—whether they're into true crime or motivational stories, there's a podcast for everyone. For example, "You love true crime, but have you heard about this unsolved mystery in space?" (Okay, not real, but it should be). And don't forget to share those priceless

moments that have you cracking up, like when you both are listening to your favorite host having a total brain freeze on-air. It's these shared giggles and gasps that make your podcast club a highlight of the week!

- Voice Notes & Variety
    - Send Voice Notes & Try New Activities: After watching a show, hearing a song or listening to a podcast, send a quick voice note sharing your thoughts. Hearing your excitement or surprise adds a personal touch that texting can't capture.
    - Keep Conversations Random: To keep things fun, throw in some unexpected randomness—send a 2am text asking, "Do fish get thirsty?" and let the laughter flow. It's all about keeping the conversation playful and engaging.

- Shared Traditions & Celebration Days
    - Start a *Rec of the Week* Tradition: Every week send your friend a recommendation—a song, show, or podcast. It's like a virtual friendship gift. Then, plan a "Friendship Day" to catch up on everything you've recommended to each other, turning it into a fun, shared celebration of your interests.

When it comes to sharing moments that make you laugh, think, or groove, you're doing so much more than just filling up time together—you're creating a friendship that's bursting with joy and layers of unforgettable memories. So, load up your playlists, find a trending TikTok, and start sending those must-listen podcast links. It's about finding delight in the little things, strengthening your bond in life's inbetween moments, and showing your friend, "I'm thinking of you."

19

CELEBRATE LIKE A CHEERLEADER
Pump Up Your Friends' Wins!

Everyday moments are the heartbeat of friendship, and there's something extra thrilling about showing up for the big wins. When your friends hit milestones—whether it's acing an exam, landing a job, completing a 5K run or managing to fold a fitted sheet (seriously, that deserves an award), it's natural to feel excited for them. Not every win calls for loud chants and pom-poms. Sometimes, it's about showing up in a way that feels authentic for both of you, whether that's jumping around in excitement or offering a quiet nod of approval. Wins come in all shapes and sizes, and so should the celebrations.

It's the Little Wins, Too

Surviving a Monday without spilling coffee counts as a win in my book. So why save all the excitement for the big stuff? Sometimes it's those little daily triumphs—like learning to parallel park or not killing the office plant—that need celebrating too! Whether they are ticking off items on their to-do list or finally figuring out how to boil eggs without crying, let them know you have noticed.

A quick, "Wow, you handled that like a pro! Proud of you!" can turn an ordinary day into something memorable. It's these little boosts that can keep your friends' spirits lifted and motivated.

Share in Their Excitement

One of the best ways to acknowledge a win is by letting your friend's excitement be contagious. If they are buzzing on adrenaline after a big achievement, join them on that wave! Maybe you are not planning a parade, but a heartfelt "Look at you go!" can be just as powerful.

Whether they've just finished a marathon (or watched a marathon of their favorite show—both are hard work), let them bask in the glow, and join in with your own version of celebration. Extra credit if you're right there by their side, toasting to their success.

Be Their Biggest Motivator

It's easy to cheer on friends when they're riding high, but what about when they're in a slump? Sometimes, the best way to celebrate future wins is by reminding them of past victories. "Remember when you thought you couldn't survive a week without takeout, but you meal-prepped for five days straight? You can handle this!" Offering encouragement during tough times keeps the momentum going and builds resilience, so when they hit their next win, they will know you've been there all along.

Keep It Simple, Keep It Genuine

Celebrating wins doesn't have to mean throwing a party every time. Sometimes, the best way to mark a friend's success is through those quieter, shared moments—a cozy dinner, a night in with snacks, or toasting with a glass of bubbly. It's not about the size of the celebration but the quality of the connection. Being a supportive friend means cheering on the journey rather than waiting for the big finale. So, bring the good vibes, notice the little victories, and let each celebration feel as unique and genuine as the friendship itself!

From Promotion to Celebration

Leaving the tech company I had spent 19 years at was a huge shift for me—it felt like leaving a family I had grown up with. Making the leap to a new company was exciting and nerve-wracking, and from day one, it felt like the right move. The environment was vibrant, collaborative, and full of positive energy—like being welcomed with a big, warm hug. The team was focused and driven, and even though we worked long hours, there was a shared passion for what we were doing that made every bit of the effort worthwhile.

When I started, I took on more than I initially expected, diving into projects and responsibilities left and right. I wanted to make an impact, and soon, it paid off. My leadership team recognized my efforts and handed me a promotion to Director—a position I had only dreamed of. It felt surreal. I cried, I laughed, and I toasted to my success like I had just unlocked the ultimate level in a video game.

In the days that followed, I shared the news with a few close friends. Their reactions were incredible. Suddenly, flowers were delivered to my doorstep, congratulatory cards arrived, I received cookies, and even a surprise Starbucks coffee landed in my hand. Their excitement for my success was contagious. Honestly, their joy was probably more thrilling than the promotion itself. It reminded me of how meaningful it is to have friends who truly *celebrate* with you—not just politely congratulate you but jump in with both feet and cheer you on with everything they've got.

Inspired by their kindness, I've made it a point to reflect that energy. When my friends face significant moments—whether it's buying a home, adopting a dog, landing a new job, or mastering a new recipe—I'm right there cheering them on. I throw mini-celebrations for every achievement, big or small, because it's essential to acknowledge those wins. Whether it's sending a congratulatory text, organizing a casual get-together, or simply giving a heartfelt shout-out, I believe that every step forward deserves recognition. Just like my friends did for me, I want to be the one who lifts them up and reminds them how far they've come.

That shared joy is what makes victories even sweeter. And when you cheer for others, it creates a cycle of support that lifts everyone up.

Win-Win Friendship Tactics

- **Be Curious & Mirror Their Energy:** Go beyond the basic *Congrats!* and ask questions that get them talking about their journey, like "What part of this process made you feel like a boss?" or "Which victory snack are we ordering tonight?" Mirror their excitement, too—whether it's raising a coffee mug or jumping up and down with them. Reflect their energy with, "You did WHAT? That's huge!" It keeps the convo flowing and adds more flavor to the celebration.

- **Celebrate the Big & Small Wins:** Don't wait for huge milestones to offer positive affirmations. Drop little reminders like, "You've been on fire lately—keep crushing it!" Even when your friend's not the party poppers type, a low-key "You are absolutely thriving! I'm quietly fist-pumping for you" text can be just as meaningful.

- **Acknowledge Progress & Past Wins:** Recognize the small steps they're taking, and say, "I've noticed how much effort you've put into this—it's inspiring!" If they hit a rough patch, remind them of their past wins with a boost like, "You've handled tougher stuff before—remember when you nailed that deadline?"

- **Surprise & Support Along the Way:** Surprise your friend with small gestures—an encouraging GIF, a goofy note, or even "You're nailing life right now" on a sticky note can brighten their day. Keep the positive vibes going by checking in after the initial celebration, like "How's that new project going?" Show them you're in it for the long haul. And don't forget that after your friend reaches a milestone, encourage them to keep going. Say, "This is only the beginning—what's next for you?"

When you commemorate your friends' wins, you create a ripple effect. Your energy lifts them up, and in turn, they'll do the same for others. It's not always about planning elaborate celebrations; it's about fostering a culture of support that strengthens your tribe. So, whether you're doing a happy dance, quietly texting your congratulations, or mentally tossing confetti, keep celebrating those wins, big and small. Remember, it's the little moments of joy that often mean the most, turning ordinary days into unforgettable memories.

20

CREATE SHARED ADVENTURES
Turn Moments into Memories!

Hey now, we aren't just about cheering from the sidelines—we are jumping into the action too! Nothing brings friends closer than diving into fun and spontaneous experiences together! You might be planning an epic weekend trip, tackling a group fitness challenge, or simply finding hobbies you both enjoy, shared adventures are where friendships truly grow and develop. These moments turn into the stories you will laugh about for years basically, the stuff of legends.

Think about it. Remember that time your "quick hike" turned into a three-hour trek because someone *definitely* knew the way (but didn't)? Or the time your road trip playlist included so much '90s boy-band music you all swore to never speak of it again? These are the kinds of stories that bond friends for life. So, why not mix it up with new adventures? Plan a weekend camping trip, conquer an escape room, or even have a low-key beach day that somehow turns into a sandcastle competition. Trust me, it doesn't have to be fancy to be unforgettable.

Let's Mix It Up!
Looking to shake things up? Why not dive into something totally new? Take a cooking class where you all *try* not to burn the soufflé, sign up for a 5K even though no one has run since high school, or brave a rumba dance class. Not only will you walk away with new skills (or entertaining fails), but you will also have stories that will be retold for years. And for those of you who want to take it up a notch, how about a themed karaoke night where everyone sings as their favorite cartoon character?

Make Memories That Matter
Of course, adventures don't always have to be about who can sing the worst rendition of a Spice Girls song. Why not add a little heart to the mix? Get your squad together and volunteer for a cause you all care about. It's a win–win: You bond over the experience while doing some good in the world. It could be something as simple as volunteering at an animal shelter or planning a charity walk, but either way, it'll make your friendship feel even deeper and more meaningful.

Stay Close from Coast to Coast

Even if your bestie lives on the other side of the country (or world), you don't have to miss out on shared adventures! With the power of the internet (and a good Wi-Fi connection) why not plan a virtual museum tour or take part in an online course together? You can even make a digital vision board for your friendship goals or take on a month-long challenge that you can both tackle together, like a mindfulness practice or creative project. Virtual adventures offer a creative and interactive way to stay connected, no matter where everyone is.

Traditions in the Making

What's better than a random adventure? A *regular* random adventure! Turn your favorite activities into full-blown traditions. Whether it's an annual trip to the same beach spot, or a post-hike pancake feast (because who *doesn't* deserve carbs after that?), traditions keep everyone coming back for more and give your friendship some serious longevity. Who knows? Maybe years from now, you will still be laughing about wearing outrageous onesies during your movie marathons.

Creating Lasting Memories: A 50th Birthday Retreat to Remember

Recently, I had the joy of witnessing something truly special—a group of lifelong friends coming together to celebrate one of our own turning 50. These amazing women have known each other since high school, and while I wasn't part of their original crew, they were visiting Arizona and graciously brought me along for the celebration. I had the opportunity to reconnect with some old friends and make a few new ones along the way.

The weekend retreat was an absolute blast. The tribe had rented a sprawling Airbnb, and from the get-go, it was clear this trip would be one for the books. Every detail was perfectly planned: from scoring rodeo tickets to bringing in a private yoga instructor for a relaxing bonding session at the house. The place was stocked with fun charcuterie boards, and everyone received personalized swag bags, which added a thoughtful touch. Some of the girls even ventured out for horseback riding, soaking up the beauty of the Arizona landscape while creating new memories together.

One of the weekend's funniest highlights? Someone brought these crazy phone cases, and one of them looked like a girl with real ponytails, which we immediately nicknamed "Darla." Darla became our unofficial mascot for the weekend, making hilarious appearances in photos—whether she was sipping wine or dominating a game of Connect 4. It was a goofy, lighthearted moment that will stay with all of us forever. Even though Darla has since been 'retired,' the memory of her antics continues to make us laugh.

What made the weekend so unforgettable wasn't the activities—it was the connection. Together, there were *hundreds* of years of shared friendship. And they welcomed me with open arms, as though I had been a part of their story all along. It was a powerful reminder that no matter where life takes us, those meaningful connections can always find their way back.

Not everyone can escape to a luxury retreat, and you don't need to. You can create these kinds of special moments right at home—pull up a YouTube yoga session, host a mixology night, or binge-watch your favorite reality show with friends. The point is to find ways to stay connected, even in small, intentional ways.

Adventure Planning 101: Planning Unforgettable Experiences

- **Plan Regular Adventures & Traditions:** Set up a standing monthly adventure with your friends, whether it's trying a new restaurant, exploring a local park, or tackling a creative project together. Regular meetups keep the laughs coming and the connection strong.

- **Be the Adventure Captain:** Don't wait for someone else to plan—step up and be the captain! Send out that group message and say, "We're doing this!" Extra kudos if it's something out of everyone's comfort zone like a pottery class or a retro arcade night.

- **Set a Group Goal:** Challenge your posse to something out of the ordinary, like conquering a climbing wall or surviving a mud run together. Win or lose, you will create a bond through the sheer ridiculousness of it all.

- **Step Outside the Box:** Suggest something completely off-the-wall, like creating your own scavenger hunt or hosting a bad movie marathon where everyone votes on the worst movie they've ever seen. (My bet: Everyone will pick something from the early 2000s.)

- **Take on a Charity Challenge:** Try a charity run or beach cleanup as a group. You'll bond over the effort, feel proud of making a difference together, and create memories that inspire even more good deeds.

- **Create a Virtual Bucket List:** Set up a list of online activities like virtual cooking classes or collaborative art projects. Tackling the list together can make even the most mundane Wednesday night feel adventurous.

- **Embrace the Little Rituals:** Start a goofy victory dance or declare that *every* group outing ends with a selfie featuring the worst "cheese" grin possible. Trust me, it'll catch on.

Don't wait—plan that next adventure, big or small, and watch how these shared experiences become the backbone that keeps friendships strong. Whether it's a beach bonfire or a random Thursday lunch, the memories you make will be replayed for years (probably with some major exaggeration). So, get out there and create those unforgettable, laugh-out-loud moments with your crew! Your next inside joke may be just one adventure away.

THROUGH THICK AND THIN
Friendship's Tough Stuff

We've all been there—whether it's dealing with the sting of gossip, trying to navigate boundaries, or figuring out how to handle the emotional weight of a friendship that's run its course. We don't talk about it enough, but friendships come with their fair share of challenges. So how do we maneuver these bumps in the road? That's what this section is all about—tackling the tough stuff head-on with a bit of reflection, a lot of empathy, and hopefully some growth along the way.

What do we say when a friend loses a parent, or when they're going through a divorce or other deeply painful experiences? Those are the times when it's hardest to know how to show up. I've worn some friends out, especially after my divorce, leaning on them too heavily. I had to realize that no single friend could take on all of my burdens. Sometimes it took journaling or finding that one friend who could handle the emotional highs and lows with me, or even seeking out a counselor to be my unbiased sounding board.

And I know each one of us has fallen victim to the dreaded mean-girl dynamic. You know the situation—when someone says, "I heard this about you," and suddenly, a game of telephone unfolds that leaves you wondering how the story got so twisted. Gossip, as tempting as it may be in the moment, has the power to hurt deeply, especially when untruths get tangled up and land in the wrong hands. Have I gossiped before? Absolutely. Have I been on the receiving end of terrible rumors about myself? Yes, and it wasn't pretty. But I'm committed to being better—to keeping secrets locked up and staying out of the toxic swirl of gossip. Protecting trust and dignity in friendships is non-negotiable.

Then, there's the need to define our personal limits. While we often emphasize this in romantic relationships, how often do we apply the same care in our friendships? Do we really understand our own boundaries, and more importantly, do we communicate them effectively? I had to learn this the hard way—not just by recognizing my own needs but also by respecting those of my friends. It wasn't until a season of tough friendship lessons that I realized I hadn't clearly defined what was acceptable for me until I was forced to face it during a period of intense upheaval. As we grow, what we're comfortable with evolves, and that's perfectly fine. The key is to understand, communicate, and live by those principles—even when it feels uncomfortable.

Sometimes, though, setting boundaries isn't enough, and we are faced with having to make the hard choice—pausing or ending a friendship. There's no guidebook to help us handle the emotional weight of these decisions, and it can feel like a huge emotional burden to bear. Maybe values just don't align anymore, or perhaps a disagreement lingers too long to move past. Whatever the case, knowing when to step back and take a break—or to walk away entirely—is crucial. My hope is to offer a bit of guidance in those moments, so we can navigate these decisions with care and kindness, both to ourselves and to our friends.

Of course, jealousy and judgment can rear their ugly heads, too. I'm the first to admit that I have to check myself when it comes to judgment—it's all too easy to slip into it without even realizing. But I remind myself: 'No shame, no blame, no judgment.' I repeat it like a mantra, because it's so important to release that need to judge and just listen to my friend's story, their beliefs and their choices. Sure, I can offer advice or insights, but if their decisions aren't hurting me, then I need to let them be. Friendship is about respecting differences, not trying to mold someone into your version of what's right.

And finally, let's not overlook the fact that it's completely natural to care deeply about two friends who don't see eye to eye. Friendships don't come in a one-size-fits-all package, and we can hold space for different kinds of connections in our lives, even when our friends don't click. Achieving harmony requires balance, respect, and the understanding that we can maintain meaningful bonds with each person, even if they don't get along with one another.

In this section, we're diving deep into these tough topics—life's storms, gossip, boundaries, breakups, jealousy, judgment, and the delicate balancing act of loving friends who might clash at times. It's not always easy, but it's absolutely worth the work to build strong, authentic friendships that can weather the storms.

21

NAVIGATING LIFE'S STORMS
Being the Rock Your Friends Need

Being a true champion for your friends means being the solid rock when life throws them into a storm. When a friend feels like they are taking punches faster than they can duck—whether it's a tough breakup, a health scare, or family drama—you become the metaphorical life vest. Your role? Be the pillar of strength that stops them from feeling like they're floating off into chaos. It's not about having the perfect words (who ever does?) but simply being there. Your presence says, "I've got you," even if you're just sitting there holding the tissues.

The "I Got You" Vibes

You are their safe harbor—a stable place to land when everything else is spiraling. Sometimes the best way to help is to sit quietly, pour a drink, and let them ugly-cry without worrying about ruining your couch cushions. It's simply *holding space*—letting them feel what they need to feel and not rushing to make things better. There's something reassuring about being that steady presence, like a reliable umbrella when the forecast says clear skies but delivers rain. In those moments, silence is a form of deep connection.

The Unofficial Therapist Role

Playing the emotional anchor can feel like running a marathon you didn't sign up for. It's hard to watch someone you love go through tough times, and it can be emotionally draining. But just by being there—through the silence or the endless venting sessions—you're lightening their load a little. Remember, it's okay to feel the weight of it all yourself. You are not a robot (unless you are, in which case, beep boop).

When a friend is going through a breakup, for instance, you might find yourself playing multiple roles: late-night sounding board, self-esteem booster, and emergency take-out delivery service. You may be there to just validate their feelings by saying, "It's totally okay to feel that way," or "Anyone would be hurt in this situation." Other times, they may need a gentle nudge to see things from a new perspective, like "What would you tell me if I were going through this?"

Another example? Maybe they're dealing with work stress and feel totally overwhelmed. Offer small, actionable support, like saying, "Why don't we take a walk and clear your head?" or "Let's come up with a game plan together." It's these little things—reminding them to breathe, letting them vent without interruption, or helping them think through solutions—that can make a huge difference.

And when you're feeling the emotional weight yourself, try setting small boundaries to recharge. You could say, "I'll be here for you, but I need a day to decompress." Taking care of yourself isn't selfish; it's necessary if you want to keep showing up as the supportive friend you are.

Finding Laughter in the Darkness

In the midst of all the heavy emotions, a well-timed joke or shared laugh can be like finding that hidden French fry in the bottom of the bag—unexpected, but exactly what's needed. The goal isn't to turn serious situations into a comedy show, but sprinkling in humor can remind your friend that brighter days and belly laughs are still ahead.

For example, if your friend is spiraling over a work mistake, you might say, "Well, on the bright side, at least you didn't accidentally reply-all to the entire company with that *let's quit and open a goat farm idea*." Or if they're feeling down after a breakup, throw in a lighthearted comment—"You know, this just means more couch space for you. Room to stretch out, right?" A little humor can ease the tension and create space for them to smile, even just for a moment.

When times are really tough—like after the loss of a loved one or a major life setback—humor can also be a gentle reminder that they're not alone. Even just saying, "I'm here, ready to make terrible puns until you feel better," or reminiscing about that hilarious shared memory can lift their spirits. Remember that inside joke about the mystery stain on their favorite sweater? You both still laugh about how it appeared out of nowhere and became an ongoing joke.

Laughter is a balm, and even in the middle of darkness, these small moments of joy remind them that they can still smile—and you're there to help them find those pockets of light.

Validation Over Verdicts

Your friend isn't looking for a life coach; they just need someone who's fully in their corner, messy emotions and all. If they're in rant mode, let them go for it without offering up solutions or a fix-it plan. Sometimes, it's simple, "That sounds so tough," or "I can't imagine how that feels, but I'm here."

This isn't the time to question their decisions or say, "Well, maybe if you had done X, things would be different." Even if you're mentally listing every way this could have been avoided, keep that to yourself. The last thing they need to feel like is they are having to defend their feelings. Instead, focus on creating a space where they can unpack all their thoughts—disorganized, emotional, or raw. Let them know their feelings are valid, even if you might not fully understand.

If they're spiraling into the same story for the third time, resist the urge to say, "Didn't we already talk about this?" Instead, try, "I know this is weighing on you. I'm here to listen as many times as you need." Little things like that make all the difference. They need someone to share the weight, not someone pointing out how heavy it is.

My Aunt's Story: Helping Francine Find the Light

Sometimes, we witness the people we care about start to drift, and it's up to us to notice the change before they sink too deep. That was the case with my aunt's friend, Francine. Normally, Francine was the life of their weekly crafting sessions, full of creativity and laughter. However there came a time when my aunt had noticed something had changed. Francine wasn't participating, and the twinkle in her eyes had dulled.

"What's wrong, Francine?" my aunt asked one day, sensing something was seriously off. Francine sighed, her voice heavy with exhaustion. "I'm just so depressed. It's all I can do to get out of bed. My life is good, my health is fine, so why do I feel like this? I should be happy, instead it's like a dark cloud follows me around, sucking the joy out of everything. Sometimes, I just want to give up."

Alarm bells went off in my aunt's head. She knew that feeling well. She had been there—stuck in the grip of depression, battling the same overwhelming darkness. She could hear the hopelessness in Francine's voice, the same uncertainty she had once felt for being depressed 'for no reason.' My aunt hesitated, unsure of how much of her own experience to share, but she thought Francine needed to hear it.

She told Francine—about living through years of loneliness and depression, and finally finding help through a psychiatrist who explained the difference between situational depression and clinical depression.

For my aunt, medication had been the key to getting her life back.

Francine listened and for the first time in weeks, my aunt saw a glimmer of hope in her eyes. Francine agreed to see the same psychiatrist. My aunt drove her to the appointment, waited in the lobby, and when Francine came out, there was a noticeable lightness in her step. The psychiatrist had confirmed that she needed help managing the chemical imbalances contributing to her depression.

That was over 20 years ago, and Francine has been a different person since. She and my aunt still meet frequently to craft, and they do it with joy, laughter, and a bond forged from navigating a dark time together. Through it all, my aunt was the lifeline Francine needed, someone who stood by her side until the storm passed.

The Art of Just Showing Up

- **Simply Be There:** Sometimes, just being in the same room, or on the other end of a call, is all that matters. A gentle "I'm here for you" says more than any advice could. Just sitting together, scrolling through puppy reels or watching cooking shows in quiet company, says *You're not alone.*

- **Hold the Space, Not the Solutions:** You don't need to solve everything. You're there to listen. If they pause or cry, it's okay to sit quietly—no words are required.

- **Check In Casually:** Drop a quick *Just thinking of you* text to remind them you care. No pressure to reply. It's like sending a virtual hug without the unease of a real one (because who has mastered the art of hugging, anyway?).

- **Validate, Don't Fix:** Offer empathy instead of answers. "That sounds tough" or "I'm here, no matter what" is often all they need to hear to feel understood.

- **Share Your Battle Scars Carefully:** If you have been through something similar, it's okay to share your experience—but don't make it a competition for who had it worse. A gentle "I've been there too" can create a bond without overshadowing their feelings.

- **When the Moment's Right Throw in Some Humor:** Laughter is a relief valve; let it happen naturally. Remind them of the inside joke about the "mystery stain" on their sweater, or let a funny memory lift the mood.

- **Respect Their Process:** Maybe they're the type to want a full-on vent, or maybe they need space. Let them handle it their way, even if that is stress-baking cookies while ignoring your calls for a week. You'll be there when they're ready.

Being a safe haven for your friend during a rough patch doesn't mean having all the right words. It means showing up, sticking around, and being that steady presence they can lean on when words fall short. By simply being there you remind them they're not alone, and that's worth more than any advice. Plus, there's always room for a joke when the moment's right—laughter really is the best medicine (well, besides actual medicine).

22

LOCK IT DOWN
Building Trust and Ditching the Drama

Being the vault for your friends means holding the master key to a treasure chest of secrets—and with that key comes great responsibility. When a friend trusts you with their most private thoughts, feelings, or that hilarious confession about their embarrassing Tinder date, you become the keeper of their inner world. Sure, the gossip might be juicy, but remember, the juicier the tea, the tighter the lid needs to stay on that kettle.

We have all been there—you are *dying* to share that ridiculously funny story your friend just dropped on you. Maybe it's a wild night out gone wrong or a confession that's too good not to share. Your group chat is screaming for this kind of entertainment, right? Wrong! Being the vault means locking it down tight, even when the urge to gossip is practically burning a hole in your phone.

The Real Weight of Trust

Trust isn't just about not spilling secrets—it's about creating a safe space where your friends feel comfortable being vulnerable. When someone confides in you, they are handing you a piece of their emotional baggage. Breaking that trust—no matter how harmless it seems—is like dropping that baggage off a cliff. Once trust is cracked, good luck rebuilding it without some serious emotional superglue. Before you spill the beans, ask yourself: Would my friend be cool with this getting out? If the answer is *NO*, then zip it up tighter than a suitcase when you're over the baggage limit at the airport.

Sharing Wisely: Processing with Discretion

Sometimes, the stuff your friends share is too big to keep inside—it might even feel overwhelming. We have also had those moments when a friend frustrates us and the temptation to vent to someone in the group is strong. But this is where things get tricky. Gossiping inside the friend group is like throwing gasoline on a campfire. It will heat things up and someone's definitely going to get burned.

Instead of opening that door, find your neutral party, someone outside your friend group who can help you process it all without fanning the flames. Think of this person as your emotional offload zone—a trusted buddy who can hear you out without starting a chain reaction of drama. They're your release valve which allows you to share the weight of the secret or frustration without betraying your friend's trust.

Building Loyalty Beyond Secrets

When your friends know they can confide in you without fear of their secrets slipping out, they're more likely to reveal their truest selves. True loyalty isn't just about keeping big, life-altering secrets; it's about being the friend who respects those confidences and creates a safe space for honesty. By holding onto their intimate details, you reinforce the foundation of your friendship.

This loyalty extends to all aspects of friendship, not just the heavy stuff. Whether you're there to support them through a wild night out that ended with a questionable hangover or lending an ear to their conspiracy theory that the new coffee shop is actually a front for an underground spy ring, every moment counts. It's in these lighter exchanges that you also solidify trust, proving that you can be both a confidant and a partner-in-crime, sharing laughs without risking the intimacy of their secrets. When your friends know you're the vault for their thoughts, it deepens the bond and ensures that every shared moment—big or small—holds a special place in your relationship.

The Cost of Broken Trust

My friend Maria had been a beloved volleyball coach for years. Her players adored her for both her coaching expertise and her radiant personality, which could light up *any* room. Behind the scenes, though, Maria was going through an overwhelming divorce, struggling to juggle her personal life with the responsibilities of leading a team.

In a moment of vulnerability, Maria confided in one of her assistant coaches—a friend she had grown close to over the years. She shared her struggles, explaining that she needed to take a few days to focus on her mental health with her parents. It was a deeply personal conversation, and Maria trusted that it would remain between them. Her trust was shattered.

Despite their friendship, the assistant coach shared Maria's private struggles with another mutual friend, whose daughter played on the team. As is often the case, the secret was passed along, and the story became exaggerated. The mutual friend took it upon herself to go to the athletic director, painting a picture of Maria's mental health spiraling out of control.

Before Maria could grasp what was happening, she was called in by the athletic director and told she'd need to undergo a series of mental health screenings to continue coaching.

Maria was devastated. A personal, private conversation with someone she trusted had blown up, affecting her career and reputation. She felt blindsided, betrayed, and humiliated. Her confidence was shattered, leaving her unfairly portrayed in a false light. Rather than receiving support and understanding, she was met with judgment and scrutiny.

Maria's experience reminds us of the responsibility we carry to handle each other's hearts with care. It's our responsibility to protect that trust, to be a trustworthy shelter when life gets tough, and to recognize that once trust is damaged, the impact can extend beyond just hurt feelings. True friendship means listening and guarding each other's vulnerabilities with the care they deserve. Let's be the kind of friends who value that trust, knowing that the strength of our bonds depends on it.

Trust-Proof Moves

- **Lock It Down:** Before you let that story slip, ask yourself: *Does your friend trust you to keep this private?* If *yes*, imagine turning that key and securing it firmly in place.

- **Phone a Neutral Friend:** When the secret feels too heavy, vent to someone totally outside the circle. This way, you process what you are feeling without risking your friend's confidentiality.

- **Stay Focused on You:** If you are feeling frustrated, focus on your own feelings instead of bad-mouthing your friend. Saying, "I'm feeling stressed about what happened" is healthier than "They always do this!" It keeps the conversation productive and helps you avoid spreading negativity.

Gossip might seem harmless, but it's the sneaky villain that chips away at trust and kicks off unnecessary drama. Instead of pouring another cup of *spill the tea*, be the friend who locks down the tea leaves. When you keep confidences, you protect the trust that holds your friendship together.

Next time your fingers are itching to send that screenshot, remember true friendships endure where secrets are safe, not shared.

23

FRIENDSHIP FENCES
Respecting Boundaries with Love

How often do we talk about boundaries in romantic relationships? A lot! Almost as much as communication, but honestly, they are just as crucial in friendships. If we don't set clear boundaries, even with our closest pals, things can get messy fast. Setting boundaries doesn't mean you're building a brick wall or going full-on no entry. You're creating a healthy framework that allows you to show up as your best self while also honoring your friends' needs. Imagine putting up a friendly picket fence, not a fortress.

Protecting Your Peace
Setting boundaries in friendships isn't just about drawing lines—it's about protecting your emotional space while still being there for the people you care about. One of my closest friends was in a relationship that became a constant storm of emotional abuse and addiction issues. Throughout those months, I had been her support system, listening and offering advice through each tumultuous breakup and eventual reunion. Then as their toxic cycle continued, I started to notice a change in myself. Every time she called to talk about the latest fallout, I felt the anxiety and exhaustion growing. I wanted to be there for her, but the emotional whirlwind was beginning to take its toll on my own mental health.

I would spend hours on the phone, listening to her recount the same arguments, the same betrayals, the same heartbreak, over and over. I tried to help, to give advice, but it became clear that nothing was changing. As much as I loved her, being her constant emotional crutch was starting to drain the life out of me. I found myself feeling resentful and frustrated after our conversations, which wasn't fair to either of us.

Finally, after one particularly intense conversation, I realized something had to change. I needed to set a boundary—not because I didn't care, but because I did. I gently told her that while I would always be her friend, I couldn't continue to be the sounding board for the toxic ups and downs of her relationship. I explained that I would support her from a distance, but for my own well-being, I couldn't keep absorbing the emotional weight of her struggles.

It was one of the hardest conversations I've ever had. I was terrified she would feel abandoned, or that our friendship would fall apart. But to my surprise, she understood. She respected my boundary and even thanked me for being honest. While it didn't fix her romantic relationship, it did give me the emotional space I desperately needed to recharge and maintain my own mental health.

By setting those boundaries, I was able to be a better friend in the long run, without sacrificing my own inner peace. It's a delicate balance, and one that's essential for keeping friendships strong and healthy. Sometimes, loving from a distance is the best way to care for yourself and the people you hold dear.

Know Your Boundaries First
Before we can even think about communicating boundaries to others, we have to identify our own. This starts with a little self-reflection: What are your non-negotiables? What leaves you feeling drained, frustrated, or uncomfortable? Maybe you need some alone time to recharge, or maybe you enjoy spontaneous late-night calls from one friend but not from everyone. Knowing where you draw the line is essential before you can explain it to anyone else.

Recognizing your own feelings and setting boundaries doesn't mean you are rejecting your friend(s)—it ensures that your emotional and personal harmony stays intact. By understanding your limits, you'll be better equipped to show up as a supportive friend, without feeling resentful.

For example, your friend's occasional venting session? Totally cool. But if every convo turns into a never-ending spiral of doom, it's time to set some limits as it can leave you feeling emotionally exhausted. You could say, "I love being here for you, but let's mix it up with some lighter topics. I need a break from the gloom!" Because honestly, no one signed up to be an all-hours crisis hotline.

And then there's the friend who always brings the storm clouds (think Eeyore here). Nothing is ever sunny in their world. You want to help, but you can only absorb so much negativity. Try gently setting a boundary by saying, "I care about you, but I also need to protect my own energy. I'm here for you, but maybe we don't let every convo turn into a *woe-is–me* saga."

This isn't about shutting people out. This is when you honor yourself and create space for relationships that truly enrich your life. When you set boundaries based on your values, you make room for meaningful connections, rather than feeling obligated to show up in ways that drain you. Saying *NO* when something doesn't align with your needs or beliefs is empowering, and it allows you to show up authentically in the friendships that matter most.

Communicate with Clarity

Once you know your boundaries, it's time to talk about them, because as much as we might wish, friends still aren't mind readers. It might feel uncomfortable, like asking for an extra side of ranch dressing and wondering if it will cost you more. Trust me, it's worth it. Be clear, kind, and direct. For instance, instead of saying, "Stop calling me late at night," try, "I love our chats, but I really need evenings to wind down. Can we catch up earlier?" Just like I did with my friend, explain why you need to set the boundary in a way that shows you still care. "I love you, but I need to take care of myself, too" goes a long way.

The key here is balance—you want to communicate your needs without making your friends feel like they're walking on eggshells. It's a shared journey, and just as you have boundaries, your friend has theirs, too. Boundaries are about teamwork—both sides respect them, and everyone wins.

Respecting Their Boundaries, Too

So, while we are busy setting our own boundaries, it's important to remember that our friends have them too. Maybe they are the friend who doesn't drink, the one who is super private and doesn't want to share every detail of their life, or the one who doesn't like to talk before 8am or after 7pm. Whatever their boundary is, it is crucial that we respect it just as much as we expect them to respect ours.

Respecting each other's limits makes for healthier, stronger friendships. When a friend sets a boundary, listen—do *not* take it personally. Boundaries are about what people need to feel safe, supported, and balanced in their relationships, not a reflection of how much they care about you. By honoring your friend's boundaries, you are showing them that you value their well-being just as much as your own.

Consistency Is Key

Maintaining your boundaries is just as important as establishing them. Upholding your boundaries consistently is crucial; otherwise, they lose their effectiveness. If you express the need for alone time but respond to every single midnight text, your boundary becomes as useful as a chocolate teapot. Stay firm! Boundaries are like a well-tuned instrument—they only hit the right notes when you practice them regularly.

Boundaries Change as We Grow

As we grow, so do our boundaries. What worked for you five years ago might not work now, and as your life changes, your boundaries will too. Regularly checking in with yourself to re-evaluate what you need from your friendships is key. And don't be afraid to adjust your boundaries when necessary. Growth is a part of life, and your relationships should evolve with you.

Boundaries in Action: We've All Been There— Examples

- **The Non-Drinking Friend:** You love happy hour, but your friend doesn't drink. Instead of pushing them, suggest an activity you can both enjoy—"Mocktails and movie night?"

- **The Friend with the Abusive Boyfriend:** Supporting a friend in a toxic relationship can be draining, and it's important to set limits. Let them know you're there for them, but make sure you're protecting your own emotional energy too. Be supportive, but don't let their situation be consuming. Set a limit on how much time you can dedicate to that conversation.

- **The Friend Who Never Lets You Get Off the Phone:** We have all got that friend who can talk for hours. Set a clear boundary by saying, "I've got 15 minutes before I need to run some errands, but I'd love to catch up!" That way, you are managing expectations upfront.

- **The Friend Who Gets Too Political:** You and your friend might have vastly different views on politics, and every time the topic comes up, things get heated. To keep the peace, you could set a boundary by saying, "I love our conversations, but politics always gets too intense for me. Can we keep that topic off-limits."

Your Guide to Healthy Boundaries

- **List Your Non-Negotiables:** Take some time to write down 3-5 boundaries that are crucial for your emotional well-being in friendships. Write it down so you are clear on what matters.
    - ✓ **Necessary Alone Time:** Prioritize personal downtime for recharging.
    - ✓ **Keep It Within Hours:** Limit calls and texts to agreed-upon times.
    - ✓ **Respect for Opinions:** Foster a culture of mutual respect in discussions.
    - ✓ **No Gossip:** Maintain supportive and positive conversations.
    - ✓ **Quality Over Quantity:** Value meaningful interactions over frequent hangouts.
    - ✓ **Emotional Availability:** Ensure friends are present and supportive when needed.
    - ✓ **Support for Growth:** Surround yourself with friends who encourage your personal development.

- **Check In with Your Energy Levels:** Pay attention to how you feel after interacting with friends. If you notice recurring feelings of frustration or exhaustion, it might be a sign that you need to establish clearer boundaries.

- **Speak Up & Set the Tone**
    - ○ **Using Those "I" Statements to Communicate:** When setting a boundary, remember to use the "I" statements to keep the focus on your feelings. For example, "I need some quiet time in the evenings" instead of "You're always calling at the wrong time."
    - ○ **Practice Saying No:** If you struggle with setting boundaries, practice saying *No* in low-pressure situations.

Try declining small things, like skipping a coffee date when you are tired, to build confidence in protecting your time.

- **Tune into Their Needs**
  - **Ask About Their Boundaries:** Don't guess—ask! "How do you like to stay in touch?" or "Anything that makes you uncomfortable in our convos?" This opens up the dialogue and shows you care.
  - **Respect Their Signals:** Pay attention when friends drop hints about their boundaries. If they are saying, "I need a break," or pulling back from certain topics, respect their needs without pushing further.

Setting these boundaries is about crafting a zone of trust where you and your friends remain unbreakable. These guidelines allow you to express yourself freely without feeling overwhelmed, and they demonstrate to your friends that you care enough to be honest. Establishing these personal lines shows respect—for yourself and for those you cherish. It's not always easy, but trust me, your friendships will thrive as a result.

24

PRESS PAUSE
When It's Time to Take a Break from a Friendship

What happens when boundaries aren't enough, and the friendship starts feeling like your barista messed up your coffee order, and you end up with a too much foam. And just like your coffee, sometimes friendships need a little stir to get things back on track. When tensions rise, morals clash, or you feel like you are about to lose it over one more passive-aggressive comment, it's perfectly okay to give yourself permission to hit the pause button. Taking a break doesn't mean you're abandoning ship—it means you're docking the boat for repairs.

Hitting Pause Isn't the End

Sometimes, after a heated debate (like whether pineapple belongs on pizza) or when your friend's tough love starts to feel more like unfiltered opinions, pressing pause can prevent you from saying something you can't take back. It's not about slamming the friendship door shut; it's more like gently closing it for some peace and quiet. Like hitting *mute* during a Zoom meeting—you just need a minute to breathe.

Taking a break gives each of you the space to cool down before things spiral out of control. You are protecting the foundation, ensuring that if and when you're ready to reconnect, the bond isn't shattered. And remember, pressing pause isn't a sign of weakness—it's a sign of maturity. It shows that you value the friendship enough to give it the chance to repair and recover rather than letting frustrations pile up and damage it *beyond* repair.

Taking a Time-Out

Set a timeframe for yourself so that your pause doesn't turn into a never-ending vacation. It could be a couple of weeks, a month—whatever you need to get some clarity. Just don't let it drag out indefinitely, or your friend might start wondering if the friendship got lost in the Bermuda Triangle.

Taking a break is not the same as breaking up. It's more like saying, "I love you, but right now, I just can't deal with your commentary on my life choices." So, don't be afraid to hit pause when needed. Sometimes, stepping back is the only way to move forward, stronger and with a deeper understanding of each other.

Use this opportunity to reflect on what the relationship means to you and what you genuinely want moving forward. Are there specific behaviors that triggered the need for a pause? What boundaries can help prevent similar situations in the future? Jotting down your thoughts can provide clarity and set the stage for a productive conversation.

Moving Forward without a BFF Meltdown
After taking that necessary 'pause', you can consider how to proceed in a healthier way. That pause can feel like hitting the gym after a long break—it's a little tough, but oh–so necessary. Just like you wouldn't try to lift the heaviest weights after taking months off, don't dive back into your friendship until you have given yourself enough space to cool down and reflect.

When you're ready to connect, approach the reunion with a spirit of openness. Share what you've learned during your time apart. For instance, maybe you realized how much you truly value the friendship or discovered that certain topics are best left untouched. Be honest about your feelings, and express your desire to understand your friend's perspective. This approach transforms the reunion from a potential confrontation into a collaborative dialogue.

Inject some humor into the situation! Yes, I am all about the laughter. Lightening the mood with a shared laugh can break the tension. Maybe joke about how you had to binge–watch that new series alone or how you've taken up an unusual hobby to fill the void. Laughter is an incredible bonding tool and can help you ease back into the friendship, reminding both of you of the joy that brought you together in the first place.

Celebrate the opportunity for a fresh start. Acknowledge the bumps along the way and use them as building blocks toward a stronger friendship. Remember that working through conflicts can lead to deeper intimacy and trust, provided both of you are willing to put in the effort. After all, friendships are like fine wine—they can improve with age, especially when they're nurtured with understanding and care.

Finding the Way Back: Reviving a Friendship on Hold
Charlotte and I met not long after my divorce—one of those unexpected

connections that just clicked. She was my hairdresser, and I was the lonely girl in the chair, and we quickly became friends, sharing laughs, long talks, and life's hysterical moments. Over the years, we built some beautiful memories together, from weekend hangouts and wine nights to our shared love of R&B.

About a year ago, things started to change. I moved to Arizona, and Charlotte found herself in a new romantic relationship. Slowly, we began to drift apart. I'll be honest—I had been wearing her down by repeatedly bringing up the same issues with my partner, stuck in a cycle she'd heard before, hoping for a different outcome. Looking back, I completely get it. I wasn't seeing the effect my romantic issues were having on her.

It wasn't a dramatic falling out—no big fight or heated words. We just both took a step back, and our conversations slowed to a stop. It hurt a little, but in hindsight we both knew it was time for a pause. About eight months went by before we started texting again, and at first, it was just the occasional message, something funny or a meme that reminded us of each other. Nothing too deep, just light exchanges to remind one another that we were still in each other's thoughts.

Then one day, she called. I was honestly so delighted—I didn't expect it. She had an amusing story to share, and I was the only one who would truly understand the humor. We laughed for hours that night, picking up as if we'd never missed a beat. After that, we spoke more frequently, and eventually, we revisited the past, talking through what had happened. It wasn't an easy conversation, but it was filled with kindness and mutual understanding. We aired our concerns, cleared the air, and agreed to renew our friendship.

The highlight? Not long after that conversation, Charlotte made a trip to Arizona to celebrate a very monumental birthday with me. It felt like no time had passed—we were back to our old selves, cracking inside jokes, jamming to our favorite throwback hits, and perfecting our selfie game. It wasn't just a friendship revived—it was a friendship renewed, stronger and more honest than ever.

Taking a Pause with Purpose

- **Check In with Yourself First:** Before you throw the friendship into timeout, take a sec to ask yourself what's really bothering you. Is it the *new mom* phase they are in, where you are hearing about diaper brands more than anything else? Has it been simmering for months? Write it out, so you know whether this is hiccup or a full-on emotional flat tire.

- **Take the Break Gracefully:** When things feel tense, remember to step away with the same grace as when declining a third piece of cake.—"I'm not cutting ties. I just need a little break, and a little space to process some things. I still care about our friendship and want to reconnect later." It's like telling them you need a commercial break instead of canceling the show entirely.

- **Set a Timeframe for Reflection:** It's easy for a pause to become a full-on ghosting situation. Set a deadline to check in—whether with your friend or to reflect on your own feelings—it might be two weeks or two months—so you know when it's time to decide to reconnect or continue the break. Think of it like setting an alarm for your emotional snooze button.

- **Revisit with Fresh Eyes:** When the time feels right to reconnect, don't come in guns blazing with a list of grievances. Approach things with a chill attitude—"Hey, remember that thing we were stressing about? Let's talk it through." It's not about winning an argument; it's repairing the foundation of your friendship with an open mind.

- **Make Space for Growth:** Use the time apart to grow as individuals, so when you do reconnect, it's with more understanding and less resentment. When you come back, think of it as hitting *refresh* on your browser—sometimes all you need is a *reset* to get things working again.

Pressing pause on a friendship isn't about avoiding the hard stuff. It's about giving your friend and yourself the breathing room to come back stronger. Think of it like pausing your favorite show in the middle of an intense scene. You don't stop because you've lost interest; you stop to regroup, change into your PJs, and come back ready to dive in with fresh eyes. So, when things get a little overwhelming, don't be afraid to hit that pause button, knowing you'll return with a clearer perspective and, a stronger connection.

25
WHEN A FRIENDSHIP REACHES ITS SEASON
Knowing When It's Time to Let Go

What if you hit pause and realize you don't want to hit the play button again? Friendship breakups—no one talks about them, but they can be just as tough (if not tougher) than romantic breakups. We pour so much into our friendships, and when they start to drift or feel off, it can be hard to admit that maybe it's time to part ways. But the stark reality is not every friendship is meant to last forever. Some friends are in our lives for a season and when their season is over, you don't have to storm out with a dramatic "WE'RE DONE!" It can be a graceful exit, complete with fond memories and no uneasy encounters at the grocery store.

The Slow Drift

Many times, it's not a dramatic blow-up that signals the end of a friendship—no epic text wars or slammed doors. It's more of a slow drift. Life gets busy, priorities shift, and suddenly you are no longer on the same wavelength. Conversations that once flowed like your favorite happy hour cocktails now feel like you're pulling teeth. You catch yourself wondering, do I really need to hear another story about their *pet's* workout routine? Am I the only one texting first, again? If hanging out with them feels more like an obligation than fun, it might be time to accept the friendship is fading faster than a TikTok trend.

So, how do you know when it's time? Start by checking in with yourself. Do you feel drained after hanging out with this friend? Are you constantly the one making an effort? Or maybe you have both grown in different directions, and what used to bring you together doesn't quite click anymore. If you are feeling like the friendship is more work than joy, it might be a sign that it's time to step back.

Letting It Fade (Gracefully)

Ending a friendship doesn't require a big breakup text or a "please turn in your friendship card" speech. In fact, most of the time, it's more about gracefully letting things fade without any bitterness. Think of it as acknowledging that the friendship served its purpose for a while, and now it's time for both of you to move forward in different directions. Then focus your energy on friendships that lift you up rather than ones that make you want to fake a dentist appointment to get out of plans.

When to Have "The Talk"
Every so often things get messier, and you *do* need to have *the talk*. If there has been tension or a clear conflict, then an honest convo might be your best bet to clear the air. Approach it like you're talking to an old friend (because, you know, they were your friend once). Instead of blaming them, say something like, "I've noticed we've been growing apart, and I just want to be honest about how I'm feeling." Cue the emotional symphony.

A Friendship Lost and Found: Letting Go with Grace
Over the years, my friend Andrea has shared stories of an on-again, off-again friendship that felt like a constant emotional teeter-totter. They had been inseparable throughout high school, drifted apart during college, and then reconnected in their 20s, spending weekends together like no time had passed. But as they entered the phase of raising children, their paths began to diverge. Their values clashed—everything from fast food vs. organic diets to vaccinating vs. not vaccinating, and each conversation seemed to turn into a debate about who was right or wrong.

They would often take breaks from one another, sometimes for six months, sometimes a year, thinking space would heal the rift. But each time they reconnected, a new disagreement surfaced—this time about politics, another time about their kids' schools (private vs public). The final straw came when Andrea was going through an unexpected separation from her husband, a time when she needed support the most. Instead of offering a shoulder to lean on, her friend called repeatedly, not to comfort, but to gossip, digging for details to spread to anyone who would listen. It became painfully clear that the friendship was no longer based on mutual respect, but rather had devolved into a one-sided relationship where trust had eroded.

After 30 years, my friend made the hard but necessary decision to let go. She pulled back, stopped responding, and created the emotional space she needed to move forward. She could still remember the good times, like their high school adventures and their years of weekend hangouts, but she also recognized that clinging to the past was no longer serving her well-being. She understood that friendships, just like any relationship, need to evolve and grow in healthy ways, and sometimes letting go is the most loving thing you can do for yourself.

Letting go of a friendship that has run its course is never easy, but it opened the door for her to create space for new, more aligned connections in her life, ones that reflected her values, supported her growth, and gave her the genuine love and care she deserved. Sometimes, knowing when to let go is the best way to honor the journey you've had with someone, while also honoring the journey ahead of you.

Moving On with Care

- **Assess the Friendship: Self–Check and Dynamics**
    - **Conduct a Self-Check: Ask yourself:** Do you feel energized or drained after spending time together? Are you mentally plotting your escape before dinner is even over? Does it feel like you're investing more than you're receiving? If you're left feeling depleted or disheartened, it might be time to reassess the friendship.
    - **Observe the Dynamics:** Pay attention to whether the friendship has become one-sided. Are you always the one reaching out, or do conversations feel forced? If it feels like you're holding up a tent that's ready to collapse, it may be time to step back.

- **Detach Gracefully & Plan Honest Conversations**
    - **Graceful Detachment:** If you've realized that the friendship no longer sparks joy (thanks, Marie Kondo), let it fade naturally. Ease up on initiating plans and focus on relationships that leave you feeling uplifted. This allows the friendship to dissolve without bitterness.
    - **Plan an Honest Conversation:** If there was a specific conflict or tension that had built up, once again use "I" statements like, "I've felt us drifting apart," to avoid making it a courtroom drama. Approach the conversation with kindness, like "I've noticed we haven't been clicking lately, and I'd love to talk." This can help provide closure without hard feelings.

- **Welcome Change & Make Space for New Connections**
    - **Recognize the Seasons of Friendship:** Not every friendship is meant to journey through every chapter of your life. Instead of fighting to keep it going, acknowledge the shift and say to yourself, "It's been fun, but I'm ready for new chapters and new friends."
    - **Leave Room for New Friendships:** By letting go of friendships that no longer serve you, you're making space for ones that do. Think of it as clearing out your closet—you're creating room for the new (and hopefully stylish) connections to come.

Letting go of a friendship doesn't mean you have to throw away all the good memories. Think of it as closing a chapter in a really great book—it was good while it lasted, but now it's time to move on to the next one. Sometimes, friendships are like seasonal Starbucks drinks—great for a while, but they don't last forever (looking at you, Pumpkin Spice). You can move forward without the bitterness, knowing that the friendship served its purpose during its time.

FRIENDS OR FRENEMIES?
Managing Jealousy and Hidden Tension

Jealousy can seep into even the strongest friendships. Whether you're the one feeling envious or on the receiving end, it can create tension. But here's the silver lining: Jealousy doesn't have to wreck your friendships. In fact, when handled with care (and maybe a touch of humor), it can actually lead to greater empathy and insight. So, how do you handle jealousy without losing the friendship?

When You're the Jealous One

We've all had that moment—you're scrolling through Instagram, and there's your friend, living the dream while you're sitting in your pajamas eating cereal for dinner. Whether it's the impeccable home decor, the romantic getaway, or that annoyingly perfect relationship, it can make you want to throw your phone across the room. Jealousy sneaks up on you like the popcorn kernel stuck in your teeth—it's small, but man, it's irritating and just won't go away. The key is to recognize jealously without letting it spiral into something bigger.

Instead of stewing in your feelings, ask yourself: What's really going on? Am I feeling stuck in my career? Do I need a break from adulting for a bit? Once you pinpoint the cause, you can channel that jealousy into motivation—because if your friend can thrive, so can you! And hey, you can still cheer for them while plotting your own rise to glory.

When You're on the Receiving End of Jealousy

So there you are living your best life, and suddenly you notice your friend's vibe is *off*. They're not cheering for your wins like they used to, and when they do comment, it's with a passive-aggressive "Must be nice" or the dreaded "Oh, you're doing that now?"—a compliment wrapped in a skeptical glance.

First, recognize that their jealousy is likely about them, not you. It's often a reflection of their own insecurities. Instead of letting it sting, try to respond with empathy. You might say, "I've noticed you seem a little off lately—what's going on?" Opening the door for a conversation helps ease the tension and might even strengthen your bond. But if your friend starts throwing more shade than compliments, it's okay to create some space, a protective bubble around your happiness.

When Jealousy Goes Both Ways

Jealousy can often be mutual—you're envious of your friend's success, and they're feeling the same way about yours. When both of you are dealing with insecurities, it can create an emotional distance that's hard to bridge. It's like you're both playing emotional tug-of-war, and no one's winning.

In these situations, open communication is your best friend. Acknowledge the awkwardness head-on. You might say, "I've been feeling a little envious lately, and I realize it's been affecting how we interact. How are you feeling?" Creating space for both of you to express emotions helps clear the air and fosters mutual understanding, leaving you both feeling better.

Green-Eyed Monsters & Coffee Chats

Maria and Dani had been thick as thieves since college—two peas in a pod who could finish each other's sentences and laugh at the most ridiculous inside jokes. They had been there for each other through all the highs and lows of life: the bumpy dating phases, job hunts, and late-night pizza binges. When Maria landed her big promotion—one she'd been working towards for years—she couldn't wait to tell Dani. She expected the same reaction Dani had whenever something great happened: excited squeals, a million emojis in their group chat, and maybe even a celebratory cocktail or two.

But that didn't happen. Instead, when Maria shared the news, Dani's responses were...off. Instead of the usual, *OMG, I'm so proud of you!* Dani's congratulations came with a side of passive-aggressive comments like, "Guess some people just have all the luck, huh?" or "Wow, you've really got it all figured out."

Maria started feeling uneasy. She'd always been able to count on Dani's support, and now, something was different. The next few hangouts with Dani were filled with tension. No matter how much Maria tried to keep things light, Dani seemed distant, throwing out little barbs that landed harder than she realized. One afternoon, after yet another *You're so lucky!* remark, Maria reached her breaking point. "Okay," she thought to herself, "I can't let this keep festering like that leftover takeout I forgot about in the fridge. Time to face it head-on."

Maria decided to tackle the issue. In true Maria fashion, she tried to break the ice with a joke. "Dani, if I didn't know any better, I'd say you're turning into a green-eyed monster. Are you jealous of my newfound fame as *Corporate Queen?*" She said it with a grin, hoping humor would soften the blow. Dani laughed nervously, but Maria could tell there was more going on beneath the surface.

After a moment of hesitation, Dani finally admitted, "Honestly? Yeah, I've been feeling a little… jealous. It's been tough at work lately. I feel like I'm stuck in the same spot, and when you got promoted, it hit me hard. Why can't I get my life together like that?"

Maria was relieved, finally, the truth was out. She reached across the table and grabbed Dani's hand. "Girl, I'm flattered you think I have it all together! Half the time, I'm one spilled coffee away from a meltdown," she joked. "I get it. I've been there. It's hard when it feels like everyone's moving forward while you're stuck in neutral. But we're in this together, remember?"

They spent the rest of the afternoon talking about Dani's work struggles and bouncing around ideas for how she could reignite her passion for her career. By the end of the conversation, the tension had lifted, and Dani was feeling inspired rather than envious.

Of course, the jealousy didn't magically disappear overnight, but it was no longer the elephant in the room. They both realized that, like a stubborn yoga pose, it takes practice, balance, and a few falls along the way to grow stronger. Instead of letting jealousy chip away at their friendship, they used it to deepen their bond—proving again that even the stickiest situations can be worked out over coffee and a good laugh.

Keeping Friendships Strong When Jealousy Creeps In

- **Self-Reflection First:** Jealousy often starts with personal feelings, so take a moment to reflect on your own emotions. Are you projecting any insecurities? Identifying the root of your feelings can help you approach the situation with clarity and empathy before addressing the jealousy at hand.

- **Talk It Out:** Whether you're feeling jealous or on the receiving end, ask your friend. "I noticed you've been critical about my career change—what's on your mind?" can shift the conversation from conflict to understanding. If certain topics bring out jealousy set boundaries. You might say, "Let's skip work talk if it's causing tension between us," to keep the conversation in safer territory.

- **Depersonalize Their Reactions:** If a friend is acting distant or snippy, remember that it's likely their own insecurities at play. Choose a calm moment to ask, "I have noticed some tension when I talk about certain things. Can we talk about what's going on?" When discussing your feelings, avoid sounding accusatory.

- **Support Each Other's Growth:** Celebrate your friend's wins and use them as inspiration for your own journey. Friendships should be a source of motivation, not competition.

- **Give Yourself & Your Friends Grace:** Jealousy is a human emotion, and it's okay to feel it from time to time. What matters is how you handle it and how you support each other through the highs and lows.

And remember, it's always a blast to celebrate each other's wins, even when that little green monster is trying to crash the party! A sincere "Cheers to you!" can turn jealousy into appreciation in no time. Plus, you know you'd want your friends rallying behind you when it's your moment to shine! So raise a glass and keep those good vibes alive!

27

LETTING JUDGMENT GO
Respecting Friends' Viewpoints without the Side-Eye

During the pandemic my friend Mary had been struggling deeply with whether to get the COVID vaccine. She had valid concerns about it and wasn't alone—plenty of people shared her hesitations. But in her circle of friends, the judgment was harsh and unwavering. While most of her friends had gotten vaccinated without hesitation, Mary's reluctance made her feel like an outsider in her own group. Things got particularly painful one afternoon when, during what she thought was a casual conversation, one of her closest friends blurted out, "Anyone who doesn't get the shot should just die." The words landed like a punch to the gut.

Mary was devastated. It wasn't just the comment itself but the fact that it came from someone she trusted. Her friend knew that Mary hadn't gotten the vaccine yet, but instead of offering support or understanding, she had unleashed this cruel judgment. It felt like her worth as a person had been boiled down to this one decision. The weight of those words sat heavily on Mary's heart. She felt isolated, judged, and deeply hurt by the people she thought would understand her struggle.

Instead of dismissing her fears, her friends turned them into fodder for judgment. It didn't matter where people stood on the vaccine debate, the issue here was the lack of empathy. Mary wasn't against the vaccine to be defiant—she had genuine concerns that no one asked her about. The casual cruelty of her friend's remark left her feeling alienated, like she no longer belonged in a group she had always felt safe with.

As the weeks went on, Mary withdrew. She stopped attending get-togethers and avoided conversations about the vaccine entirely, worried that another hurtful comment might come her way. She even stopped sharing personal things, knowing that her opinions and feelings were being judged. It was a devastating shift for someone who had always been open and honest with her friends.

Eventually, Mary and I talked about how this situation had left her reeling. She confided in me that it wasn't just about the vaccine—it was the principle. She felt like her friends had stopped seeing her as a whole person and had reduced her to a single decision, making it easy to dismiss her feelings entirely. She felt betrayed, not just by one person but by her entire group of friends who had failed to stand up for her when she needed it most.

This experience taught Mary a lot about the importance of compassion and how friendships can quickly unravel when judgment replaces understanding. Despite the hurt, she didn't lose faith in friendship itself but became more cautious about who she shared her vulnerable moments with.

Words that Wound
Even in the most positive friendships we hit a snag—judgment. We all have moments where we catch ourselves being a little critical and opinionated (come on, we've all been there), and if you want to build strong friendships, it's time to let that go. Mutual respect isn't about agreeing on everything—embrace those differences and see the value in perspectives that don't match yours. When you drop the judgment, you clear space for genuine connections, and respect starts to grow. After all, if we were all the same, we'd be as exciting as plain toast!

Everyone's on their own path, and sometimes their route involves a few detours you wouldn't dream of taking— like their obsession with running marathons at 5am (are they part human, part energizer bunny?). Respecting your friend's perspective means understanding that their life experiences shape their choices. Just because you wouldn't do things the same way doesn't mean their way is wrong. Imagine how boring the world would be if everyone had the same playlist, opinions, and vacation destinations!

Curiosity Over Critique
So, how do you keep judgment in check? It starts with self-awareness. It's crucial to catch yourself when those sneaky thoughts creep in. Maybe your friend has a different take on a situation that you find baffling or even frustrating. Instead of jumping to conclusions or dismissing their feelings, pause for a moment. Remind yourself that their perspective is as valid as yours.

Curiosity allows for growth in your friendships. When you approach conversations with an open mind, you create an environment where both parties feel heard and respected. Remember, embracing curiosity doesn't mean you have to agree on everything. It's about appreciating the richness of diverse perspectives and recognizing that these differences add depth to your relationships. The next time you feel a wave of judgment rising, take a step back and ask yourself: "What can I learn from this?" This simple shift can turn potential friction into a meaningful exchange that strengthens your bond.

Judgment Detox: Steps to Embrace Respect Over Criticism

- **Pause Before Reacting:** When you feel judgment creeping in like a mosquito at a picnic, take a beat. Breathe, and remind yourself your friend's decisions are rooted in their own experiences. Pausing keeps your reaction from turning into an unwanted facepalm moment.

- **Ask Questions Instead of Assuming:** The next time your friend shares a choice that has you blinking twice, ask questions instead of assuming they've gone off the deep end. A simple, "What led you to that?" or "Tell me more about how you got there" turns a raised eyebrow into a real convo.

- **Shift to Curiosity Mode:** Whenever judgment creeps in, flip the script by shifting to curiosity. Instead of thinking, *Why would they do that?* ask yourself, *What can I learn from this?* By turning judgment into curiosity, you keep the conversation open and invite deeper understanding between you and your friend.

- **Own Your Judgment:** Hey, we're human, and sometimes judgment slips out like a bad dance move. Own it! Try, "I may have been a bit judgy earlier, and I'm sorry. I respect your choice, even if I don't totally get it." Humility is a friendship power move.

- **Check Your Tone:** It's not just what you say—it's how you say it. You can totally disagree without sounding like an off-key note in an otherwise perfect song. Keep your tone friendly, even when discussing something you don't see eye to eye on. This helps prevent conversations from becoming confrontational and keeps the focus on respectful dialogue.

Steering the waters of friendship can be tricky, especially when judgment tries to hijack the ship. By embracing curiosity and respecting each other's differences, you're not just avoiding conflict; you're creating a rich mosaic of understanding. The goal isn't to mold your friends into your own image, but to celebrate what makes them unique. The next time you feel that judgment creeping in, take a moment to appreciate the rich diversity of perspectives around you. Friendships are like a colorful playlist—filled with different genres and rhythms that keep life interesting! Toss in a pinch of respect and a splash of curiosity, you can transform potential friction into opportunities for deeper connections, ensuring your friendships remain as dynamic as the music that plays in the background.

28

BALANCING ACT
When Friends Don't Get Along

What happens when two friends who click with you don't quite click with each other? It's like introducing your cat to your new puppy—sometimes they just hiss, hide, and need time to adjust. Despite shared values, personalities can clash, leaving you caught between friends who don't quite vibe, suddenly thrusting you into the role of referee. You're not here to hand out yellow cards or blow a whistle, though. With a little balance and maybe patience, you can keep all your friendships strong without losing your mind.

Don't Play the Middleman
First things first: You are *not* a mediator, so don't try to play the go-between. While it's tempting to help smooth things over, it's not your job to umpire every disagreement. Encourage each friend to handle their issues directly—trust me, you don't need to be a United Nations peacekeeper.

Mixing Friend Groups? Not Required
There is no rulebook saying all your friends need to be one big, happy group. If you know two friends aren't exactly BFF material, keep it simple: Plan one-on-one time with each of them separately. You wouldn't force your peanut butter-loving friend to sit through your sushi-loving friend's lecture on raw fish, right? Same concept—different food groups.

Keep Calm & Stay Out of It
It can be tough to stay neutral when you have got one friend complaining in your ear, but here's the trick—listen without taking sides. You can acknowledge their feelings without becoming a front-row spectator in the drama. You don't need to referee a fight club; instead, focus on supporting them and staying Switzerland-level neutral.

Drawing the Line with Love
Once again let's discuss those boundaries. If you find yourself stuck in the middle too often, it's time to draw the line. Let your friends know

that you care about each of them, but you will not be dragged into their disagreements. Politely remind them that you value your relationships with them equally, and bad-mouthing or drama isn't something you want to be involved in. After all, who needs extra stress?

Encourage Civility, Not Forced Friendships
If you have to bring both friends together (think birthday parties, weddings, or holiday gatherings), don't play matchmaker. They don't need to bond over the afternoon barbeque, but they *do* need to be civil. Set the tone for a positive hangout—and if things start to get tense, steer the conversation to lighter topics. You are basically their social cruise director, but with less whistleblowing and more fun.

Let It Be: Supporting without Meddling
Trying to force a reconciliation between friends who aren't ready to make amends is more likely to backfire than help. Give them space to work things out on their own terms. Your focus should be on nurturing your individual friendships and maintaining balance, not solving every conflict. Different personalities will naturally collide sometimes, and as long as your friends respect your boundaries, you can keep things chill and stress-free.

The Friendship Triangle
Whitney had two close friends, Ashley and Megan. While both played important roles in her life, their personalities couldn't have been more different. Ashley, being more introverted, preferred quiet, intimate gatherings, while Megan was a social butterfly, always planning big weekend events. At first, these differences were easy to navigate, but over time, the contrasts began to create tension between them.

One weekend, Megan hosted one of her signature lively parties. Ashley, feeling overwhelmed by the noise and the size of the crowd, made a few offhand remarks about how chaotic things were. Unfortunately, Megan overheard these comments, and they stung. She felt hurt, thinking Ashley didn't appreciate her efforts to create a fun atmosphere. Meanwhile, Ashley felt embarrassed and misunderstood, and the tension between them grew.

Whitney found herself in the middle of this brewing conflict. Both Ashley and Megan turned to her for support, but neither seemed eager to address their issues with each other. Instead of getting sucked into the drama or trying to fix things, Whitney made a conscious decision to maintain her individual connections with both friends. She spent time with them separately, respecting that they each brought something different to her life. Over time, she set clear boundaries, telling them, "I care deeply about both of you, but it's up to you to work things out."

Years later, after many individual hangouts and gradual shifts in their lives, something surprising happened—Ashley and Megan reconnected on their own. With time, perspective, and maturity, they began to see past their differences and started to appreciate what each brought to the table. They found a balance, and what once seemed like irreconcilable personalities started to complement each other in new ways.

Keeping the Peace

- **Encourage Direct Communication & Set Boundaries:** If one friend starts venting about another, gently steer them toward direct communication with a phrase like, "Why don't you talk to them directly? It might be less complicated than passing notes through me." When they do vent, keep your responses neutral—"I hear how you're feeling," or "That sounds frustrating,"—without taking sides. If things start getting intense, shift the conversation by introducing a lighter topic like, "Speaking of frustrations, did you catch the latest episode of [XYZ]?"

  And if the venting continues, set clear boundaries by saying, "I care about you both, but I'd rather not be in the middle of this." Repeat as needed, reinforcing the mantra "I'd rather stay out of it," to remind your friends where you stand.

- **Resist the Urge to Fix Everything:** It's not your job to solve every conflict. Some issues won't have immediate resolutions, and that's okay. Instead of taking on the burden, offer support by saying, "I'm here if you want to talk, but I trust you'll figure it out." This lets you remain a supportive friend without carrying the weight of their problems.

- **Plan One-on-One Time & Skip the Group Invites:** If you sense tension, plan separate outings with each friend to avoid uneasy group dynamics. "Let's grab coffee, just the two of us," can keep things drama-free.

- **Set Group Event Expectations & Redirect the Energy:** Before a group hangout, let each friend know, "Let's make this a fun time for everyone. We're keeping it light!" If things get difficult, jump in with a fun activity or suggest a new topic of conversation. Think "Hey, let's do a group karaoke!" to shift the focus.

- **Let It Be & Focus on What You Can Control:** If you feel the urge to intervene, remind yourself that it's okay for friends to have their own process. Say, "I trust you both to work this out in your own way." Focus on nurturing your own connections without getting overly involved in their tension, think "I can't fix this, but I can show up as a good friend to both." This approach allows you to stay supportive without taking on the responsibility of resolving their conflict.

Friendships can sometimes feel like a circus act, especially when personalities clash and misunderstandings arise. With a bit of finesse and a sprinkle of humor, you can maintain the balance in your relationships without losing your cool. Remember, you are nurturing each friendship individually while giving your friends the space they need to work through their differences. Embrace the value that each friend brings to the table and focus on what makes your connections special. Remember, handling both the smooth and rough patches of friendships, even when friends bump heads, can shape your perspective and strengthen your ability to foster harmony!

NEW PATHS AND SURPRISES
🦩🦩 Embracing Change Together

Life has a funny way of shaking up things and keeping us on our toes, right? One minute, you and your friend are moving through the ins and outs of single life together, and the next, they're in a committed relationship, or maybe it's you who's all boo'd up. From the whirlwind of online dating (seriously, what a wild world!) to adapting to new routines, friendships often have to weather a lot of changes. What really matters is, regardless of a new job, new hubby or new hobby (hello, swing dancing phase) your friendship can still thrive. In fact, these shifts can lead to deeper connections and shared experiences—if you're both willing to adapt.

As someone who's experienced life on both sides—single and in a relationship—I've learned that maintaining friendships through all these life stages is vital. Whether your friend is dating, married, or just taking time for themselves, it's about supporting each other and finding new ways to stay connected. I'll admit, I've been guilty of getting swept up in a relationship and unintentionally "ghosting" my friends—so I totally understand! But the truth is, we don't have to lose our besties just because romance comes into the mix.

In this section, we'll dive into the fun, the awkward, and everything inbetween. From navigating the world of dating apps to keeping the friendship alive when life gets hectic, there's plenty to explore. And let's not shy away from those taboo topics either (yes, we're talking about sex). Whether it's sharing our own experiences or learning from each other, there's always more to discover when we embrace these moments of connection and change together.

Sometimes, it's not just about dating and relationships—life throws all kinds of other fun surprises our way. Friends moving long distances, having kids, pouring their energy into passion projects, or simply needing a break from it all—it's all part of the journey. Adaptability is key to maintaining those bonds, whether you're figuring out how to stay connected with your bestie who relocated across the country or rekindling a friendship after a hiatus. Change doesn't have to mean the end; sometimes, it's just the beginning of a new chapter.

And the roommate life—both a dream and a challenge. I haven't had a female roommate since college, but raising teenagers? Ok, alright, that's another story! Living together brings a whole new dynamic to friendships, where you learn to thrive without stepping on each other's toes, figuratively and literally.

Finally, we can't overlook our workplace besties. I still meet monthly on Zoom with two of my old work friends. We've shared some amazing moments together—between the three of us, we've worked at 15+ companies combined, and despite our careers taking us in different directions, we still love to giggle and swap workplace woes. These friendships born in the office, have evolved into something more lasting and meaningful, reminding me that the bonds we form at work can stand the test of time.

Whether it's navigating the excitement of new relationships, supporting each other through life's twists, or finding a way to make space for old friends in new places, this section is all about embracing change together. Because, at the end of the day, true friendship isn't about how often you hang out— it's in showing up for each other through all the winding paths that life has in store.

29

SINGLE, MARRIED & STILL SURVIVING
Thriving through Life's Plot Twists

As we move through different stages in life, friendships inevitably evolve. Whether you're single or married, one of the biggest changes that can affect your relationships is how life transitions impact time, priorities, and energy. Life getting busier or looking different doesn't mean your friendships have to take a backseat! It means you have got to get creative and intentional about how you sustain and enhance those bonds.

Here's how single friends and married friends can keep those bonds strong—even when one of you is ordering takeout for just yourself, and the other is learning how to compromise on which side of the bed is theirs!

Embrace the Change, Don't Resist It

The one thing you can depend on in life is change. Friendships are meant to mature as we do, and one friend getting married doesn't mean the friendship is doomed to fade. In fact, this can be an opportunity to foster closeness, as long as both sides are open to adapting to new dynamics. Instead of dwelling on what's different, appreciate the fresh perspectives your friend brings to the table.

Maybe they're sharing *marriage wisdom* like how to compromise on the thermostat settings or telling you hilarious stories about their partner's latest attempt to mount a TV—You can still connect on different levels as life changes.

Adjust Expectations but Keep the Connection

If truth be told, your newly married friend may not have the same amount of free time as before. There are family commitments, shared schedules, and sometimes, new priorities. But here's the real insight: While the frequency of hangouts might shift, the *quality* of the connection doesn't have to. Being flexible and adjusting your expectations can help keep the friendship strong. Maybe you don't get to hang out every Friday night like you used to, but that doesn't mean the bond isn't there. And for married friends, this means carving out time for your single friends, even when life gets busy.

Recognizing Wins in Different Walks of Life
One of the greatest perks of friendships between single and married people is you get to celebrate totally different kinds of wins! As the single friend, don't forget to give your married buddy props for surviving their first vacation with the in-laws without a meltdown or mastering the art of picking their battles (like which way the TP goes on the holder). Married friends, don't sleep on your single friend's victories, whether they are nailing it at work or enjoying the freedom of pulling off an epic staycation filled with pillow forts and popcorn marathons.

Avoid the Pressure to Keep Up
One of the most important things to remember in friendships is that life is not a race. Just because one friend is getting married or starting a family doesn't mean you need to follow suit, and vice versa. Often, single friends feel pressure to catch up, while married friends may feel guilty for moving into a new phase. You're each on your own extraordinary path, and that's exactly how it's meant to be.

Create New Traditions Together
As life evolves, so can your traditions. Maintaining friendships through life changes doesn't have to follow the same playbook. Instead of just sticking to routine rituals, why not try something totally different that reflects where you both are now?

- **Seasonal Bucket Lists:** At the start of each season, create a bucket list of activities you want to do together, like visiting pumpkin patches in the fall or having beach days in the summer. Check off the items as you go!

- **Crafting or DIY Sessions:** Have a regular crafting night where you try out different DIY projects together. It could be anything from jewelry making or a tie-die adventure to making homemade candles, and you can celebrate your artistic flair (or lack thereof) together.

- **Flashback Fridays:** Every month, pick a Friday to revisit a favorite childhood activity—like a silly sock puppet theater, having a sleepover, or watching cartoons together. It's a fun way to reconnect with your inner child!

- **Monthly Themed Dinners:** Choose a different cuisine each month and cook a meal together. One month could be Italian, the next could be Thai, and so on.

Friendship Flex: Rolling with Life's Changes

As life changes, so do boundaries. Yup, there's the 'B' word again. Whether it's respecting that your married friend has more family obligations or recognizing that your single friend may need the freedom to pursue hobbies or interests that their married friends may not share, being mindful of boundaries is key. Married friends might need to juggle time with a partner, while single friends might have more flexibility and different emotional needs. Respecting each other and understanding that unavailability doesn't have to feel personal will go a long way to maintaining a healthy relationship.

Growing Together, Not Apart

Whitney and her friend Lisa had been besties for years. Their friendship was so strong that when Whitney got married and started looking for a house, Lisa decided to buy one right across the street. Before Whitney's pregnancy, their lives were deeply intertwined—they went grocery shopping together, hit the clubs, hiked, walked their dogs, and spent countless hours laughing and making memories. When they weren't with their significant others, they were always by each other's side.

Lisa was ecstatic when Whitney shared the news of her pregnancy. But as Whitney's due date came and went, Lisa slowly started to pull back. Whitney noticed the change but couldn't quite put her finger on why. Whitney continued to invite Lisa on walks and hikes with her newborn son, but Lisa would always find a reason to decline. As time passed, Whitney couldn't help feeling that something had shifted in their once-tight friendship.

About a year later, Lisa's partner pulled Whitney aside during a casual get-together and revealed what had been bothering Lisa. He explained that while Lisa was happy for Whitney, the changes in Whitney's life—especially the pregnancy—had been hard on her. Lisa missed the carefree days when it was just the two of them, and she was struggling with the new dynamic of Whitney's life as a mom. She didn't know how to express these feelings and instead chose to withdraw, unsure of how to maintain their bond.

This revelation hit Whitney hard. She hadn't realized how much her pregnancy had affected Lisa and was determined to rekindle their close friendship. Whitney worked to find new ways to connect with Lisa, reaching out with thoughtful gestures and invitations that weren't centered around her baby. They started planning one-on-one time—whether it was going bowling, a movie in the park, or spending time doing activities that were reminiscent of their old days, just with a different spin.

Slowly but surely Whitney and Lisa found a way to reconnect and rebuild their friendship. While things weren't exactly as they had been before, they established new traditions and found joy in their evolving relationship. Whitney's efforts to meet Lisa halfway taught her that even when life changes dramatically, friendships can still thrive with understanding, effort, and communication.

Keep that Connection Strong

- **Support Their New Chapter & Stay Curious:** When your friend shares important moments in their relationship, be a part of their road trip where detours and pit stops are part of the fun. Ask thoughtful questions like, "What's been the most surprising part of married life so far?" or "I love that for you—tell me more!" This shows you're excited to share in their experiences, big or small.

- **Celebrate Milestones & Stay Connected:** Whether your friend is adopting a new pet or celebrating an anniversary, acknowledge their milestones with a thoughtful message or a casual hangout. Even a quick *thinking of you* text or a funny voice note can go a long way to maintain your ties between bigger catchups.

- **Plan Intentional Friend Dates:** Set a monthly date on the calendar for just the two of you, whether it's an afternoon stroll, wine Wednesday, a smoothie run, or a phone call. It gives you both something to look forward to and keeps the friendship alive.

- **Reassure & Communicate Openly:** If you sense any tension or distance, offer a gentle reassurance like, "I love that we're on different journeys and learning from each other." Be open about your feelings and let them know, "I want to make sure we're still connected, even with everything going on. Your friendship is important to me."

- **Create New Traditions & Embrace Differences:** Embrace your unique paths by creating new traditions—whether it's a couples' dinner hosted by your married friend or a creative painting or pottery workshop planned by your single friend. Mix things up by suggesting different activities like axe throwing or a photography challenge. Say, "I know this sounds crazy, but let's try [insert wild idea]—it'll be an adventure!"

- **Revisit Your Roots:** Plan a nostalgia day where you recreate one of your favorite memories together from when you first became friends. Whether it's rewatching an old TV show you both loved or revisiting a favorite hangout spot, it's a fun reminder of how far you've come.

- **Respect Each Other's Time & Send Gentle Reminders:** Honor the time commitments of your friend's life stage, and say things like, "I get it! Let's plan something when things are less hectic for you." Understand that life can be demanding, and sometimes plans need to shift. Respect your friend's commitments, and if you're feeling disconnected, gently say, "I miss our one-on-one time. Let's make it a point to hang out soon." Offer an affirmation that the friendship still matters, no matter how busy life gets.

Friendships aren't like milk—there's no expiration date! Just because life is shifting doesn't mean your friendship has to sour. Think of leftovers—they're still just as satisfying the next day, maybe even better! So why not shake things up a little? Plan something totally unexpected, throw in a bit of fun, and remind each other why you are still BFFs through all of life's changes.

30

SWIPE RIGHT, SWIPE LEFT
Being Your Friends' Dating Wingwoman

Speaking of life changes, dating can definitely come with its own sways and swerves. Dating is tough at the best of times, and the world of swipes, texts, and profile pics has taken it to a whole new level. Online dating is a battlefield your friend doesn't need to navigate alone. From first-date jitters to ghosting nightmares, you're there to cheer them on, pick up the pieces, and maybe help draft their bio (because no one besides me should have *loves tacos* as their only personality trait).

Let's explore how you can support your friend through the dating labyrinth—one awkward message, bizarre profile photo, and premature "I miss you" at a time.

From Ghosts to Giggles: Surviving Dating with Your Bestie

Mary and I went through our divorces around at the same period in our lives, and while I dove headfirst into the dating pool like I was training for an Olympic event, Mary took a bit more time before she was ready to test the waters. When she finally did, I was there, armed with all the tips, tricks, and cautionary tales I had collected along the way. Honestly, we've had more laughs than I can count—especially since we've rewritten her dating bio at least 20 times. Turns out, *Loves long walks to the fridge* doesn't attract the quality crowd we were hoping for.

Every time she goes on a date, we have this little ritual. She shares her location with me, and we go full FBI-mode—she sends me the guy's full bio, home and work address, occupation, and honestly, if we could get a copy of his social security number, we'd probably throw that in too (just kidding, sort of). The post-date debriefs are the absolute BEST! We talk about everything—from who awkwardly stared at their phone the entire time like it held the secrets of the universe to who brought their mom's advice into the conversation like it was gospel. I'll help her spot the red flags —why does he have that many cats? Or the yellow flags —he's still living with his roommate from college at 40...hmm. And since Mary refuses to ghost anyone (she's too nice for that), we come up with creative, gentle ways to let people down—cue the endless text drafts where we try to balance honesty with kindness, while also avoiding any *I'm sure we'll bump into each other again* lies.

There have been times when she's wanted to swear off dating apps forever, throw her phone in a river, and live as a hermit. But, like me, Mary loves love. Even my partner has gotten in on the fun—offering his male perspective when needed (which, spoiler alert, usually involves telling Mary to *just be direct*). With him chiming in, it's like we have our own dating strategy team.

And guess what? After all the swipes, clumsy conversations, and weird dates, Mary is in a happy, thriving relationship. And every time I see her smile, I feel like I've been part of her journey. It's honestly been hilarious and heartwarming all at once. Watching her grow through the trials and triumphs of dating has reminded me that friendship is about showing up, laughing through the madness, and always being ready to offer a reality check when needed (because, let's face it, some of those profiles are *insane*). It's a reminder that dating is easier when you've got someone who can share both the laughs and the W*hat just happened?* moments.

After all, what's friendship without a little chaos, laughter, and mutual support through the swipe–right madness?

The Emotional Roller-Coaster of Online Dating
Online dating can go from the excitement of a new match to radio silence in a matter of hours. It's like strapping into a roller-coaster—thrilling at first, but then you hit that stomach–churning drop when someone ghosts you after three days of solid conversation. And who's there for the aftermath? You!

Your job is to be the safety net when your friend is feeling like a washed–up seashell. Let them vent about the cute guy who suddenly disappeared or the girl who seemed perfect until she dropped a *hey, you up?* at 2am.

- Example: "So, your latest match ghosted after talking for a week? You know, ghosting is like an emotional sneeze—unpleasant, but it passes. On to the next one!"

Dating burnout is real. After countless disappointing dates or chats that go nowhere, your friend might feel like deleting all the apps and going off the grid. Remind them that taking breaks is healthy. They can step away, recharge, and come back when they're feeling more optimistic.

- Example: "If Tinder has you swiping so much you feel like you're playing Fruit Ninja, maybe it's time for a break."

Creating the Perfect Profile

Online dating profiles can be over-the-top, and that's putting it lightly. Between the mirror selfies, gym flexes, and bios that say, *I'm fluent in sarcasm*, it's easy for your friend's personality to get lost in the noise. That's where you come in.

Help them write a killer bio, a snapshot of who they really are—fun, genuine, and without the overused *I like craft beers and cozy blankets*.

- Example: Offer a suggestion to your bestie for that bio—Sandwich savant, amateur house-plant rescuer, and expert at dodging spoilers for the latest show.

Photo SOS: Help them avoid the classic dating-app photo fails. No one wants to see a grainy bathroom selfie or a photo with their ex hilariously cropped out. Plan a fun day where you take some great shots that show off their personality.

- Example: "Let's get some real pics that say, *I'm fun and normal*, not I may or may not live in a basement."

Handling Rejections & Ghosting

Rejection and ghosting are part of the online dating game, and that doesn't make them any less brutal. Sometimes, your friend might need a pep talk after getting ghosted (again) or after a date where they felt like they were being interviewed for a job for which they didn't apply.

It's not personal: Ghosting, as painful as it is, usually has nothing to do with your friend. It's often about the other person's issues, not theirs.

- Example: "Look, if they can't see how amazing you are, they're doing you a favor by disappearing. It's like the dating universe's way of sorting the trash from the treasure."

Spotting Red Flags

Maybe your friend is head-over-heels for someone new, and everything is moving quickly. You've been supportive, but now you're seeing some red flags. It's time to gently bring them back to reality without being a buzzkill.

Keep it light and clear: You don't want to rain on their parade, but it's important to remind them to stay cautious. If they're ignoring signs of love-bombing or inconsistencies, you can ask thoughtful questions.

- Example: "Hey, they seem great, but is it normal to get a *Good morning text!* 17 times a day? Let's make sure they're not too intense too soon."

Preventing Dating Burnout

Swiping for hours, messaging five people at once, and keeping up with multiple matches can become overwhelming. When your friend starts feeling the strain of dating burnout, you're there to remind them to slow down and set boundaries.

Encourage balance. It's important to let your friend know they don't need to respond to every message immediately or go on a date every weekend. Suggest taking things at their own pace and mixing dating with self-care.

- Example: "If swiping right feels like a part-time job, maybe it's time to log off and do something that doesn't involve a screen—real-life human interaction!"

The Weird World of First Dates

First dates are nerve-wracking, but throw in a dating app, and it's a whole different level of anxiety—like trying to tame a wild raccoon! Your friend might need you to channel your inner fairy godmother, helping them prep for that first meet-up. Whether it's delivering a pre-date pep talk that rivals a pro sports coach or sifting through their outfit choices like a fashion consultant with a caffeine addiction, you're on duty.

If they ask for your opinion on what to wear, be honest and encouraging—it's not about lying, but rather about finding that balance between *You look great!* and *Are you really going to wear that?* Remember, the right outfit can turn their nervous jitters into a confident strut. When it comes to first impressions, you want them to feel like a million bucks, not a poodle in a tutu.

- Example: "You look amazing, but maybe swap the 5-inch heels for something you can run in—just in case the date is a bust, and you need a quick exit."

When They Find "The One"

Eventually, your friend might meet someone special (thank you, Bumble, for my match—four years strong!), and suddenly, they're swept off their feet. You're thrilled for them, but you also want to make sure they don't get too caught up in their new romance and forget their friendships.

Join in the joy: Be genuinely happy for your friend and remind them to keep a healthy balance between their new relationship and their other important connections.

- Example: "I'm so excited for you! Just don't forget—friendship coffee dates are still a thing."

Be the Wingwoman They Never Knew They Needed

Dating in the digital age is like trying to solve a Rubik's Cube blindfolded—full of swipes, DMs, and signals that are as clear as mud. With you as their trusty sidekick, your friend can tackle anything that comes their way. Whether they're on the hunt for *The One* or just trying to survive another first date without spilling their drink, you're right there with advice, laughter, and a healthy dose of dating-profile roast sessions that could rival a comedy special.

In the uncharted territory of online dating, nothing screams *I've got your back* louder than helping them dodge red flags like they're in an intense game of Twister and reminding them that their perfect match is out there—probably sandwiched between a guy who thinks cats are superior and a gal who believes ghosting is a valid method of communication, like a magician's disappearing act.

31

LOVE IN THE AIR
Don't Ghost Your Friends!

You've helped your friend navigate the wild world of online dating—swipes, goofy messages, and first-date disasters. Now they've found their person, and everything is great, right? Except, now, they're the one doing the ghosting! One minute you're helping them draft the perfect profile, and the next, your texts are getting left on *read*.

While we are all happy for our friends when they find love, that doesn't mean we are thrilled to be left in the dust! So, how do we avoid the classic *I'm in a relationship, see you in a few months* move?

Find That Sweet, Sweet Balance
We get it—new relationships are like discovering a new favorite restaurant. Suddenly, you can't get enough, and every spare moment is filled with romantic dinners and dreamy weekend plans. You're all in, savoring every bite of that new love, from the delicious first kiss to those late-night dessert runs. But while you're busy sharing appetizers and sipping wine with your new boo, let's not leave your friends hanging like an unread group chat.

Carve out some friend-time between date nights; it's all about balance, baby! Your friends are the ones who celebrated your single days, and they deserve a seat at the table. Balancing love and friendship isn't just possible; it's essential for keeping your social life vibrant and your heart full. After all, sharing those romantic stories over mimosas can make for the best of both worlds!

Let's Normalize the "Friend Check In"
Look, we're adults—sometimes we need a friendly nudge. If you're feeling like you've been sidelined while your friend's off in couple-land, it's time for a quick check in (no guilt trips needed!). You can keep it light and say something like, "I'm thrilled you've found your soulmate, but I miss our foodie-fueled gossip sessions. Let's pencil in some friend time before you disappear on another weekend getaway!" A little reminder that your friendship still matters can work wonders.

Group Hangouts Can Be a Win

Sometimes, blending worlds can help keep friendships strong and vibrant. Invite your friend and their new partner to group hangouts or fun events, like trivia nights or a backyard barbecue. This way, they don't have to choose between spending quality time with their new love or hanging out with their friends—they get the best of both worlds!

By incorporating their partner into your social circle, you create an opportunity for everyone to bond. It's a chance for you to get to know the new person in their life, and it can help alleviate any awkwardness. Plus, there's something undeniably fun about group dynamics; you can witness the chemistry firsthand while sharing laughs over inside jokes and playful banter.

These outings can also help your friend feel more at ease, knowing they don't have to juggle different aspects of their life. So, roll out the welcome mat for their partner and embrace the joy of expanding your circle. Fostering that sense of community will show your friend that you're genuinely happy for them.

Avoid the All-or-Nothing Mindset

Remember, your friend isn't trying to ditch you. They're just adjusting to their new relationship dynamic. Rather than going into all-or-nothing mode, where you expect them to be around all the time or not at all, try embracing the ebb and flow. Friendships change; they don't have to fade. A little flexibility and understanding can keep the friendship thriving, even if the dynamic shifts temporarily.

Drop a Friendly Reminder

Sometimes friends don't even realize they are disappearing. New love can be all-consuming, and they might not know how it's affecting their other relationships. Have a fun, lighthearted conversation about keeping balance. You can frame it as, "I'm glad you're so happy, but don't forget us little people!" It's all about keeping it playful while still making your point.

Friendships Aren't Light Switches: Don't Leave Them in the Dark

Maria had always made time for everyone. Whether it was last-minute plans or lengthy phone calls, she found a way to stay connected. When she met her new boyfriend, things changed. At first, her friends were genuinely happy for her. They saw how much joy the new relationship brought to her life, but as weeks turned into months, it felt like Maria was pulling away from them completely. Texts went unanswered, invitations were declined, and her friends felt like they were losing her to a new romance.

Holly, one of Maria's closest friends, decided it was time to talk. She missed the strong connection they once had and couldn't help feeling sidelined. During a sincere conversation, Holly expressed how much she and the others missed Maria's presence and how they felt like their friendship was slipping away. Maria listened but didn't seem to take it to heart. She brushed off the concerns, explaining how busy her new relationship kept her, and insisted that everything would go back to normal soon.

Things didn't improve. The group of friends kept trying to reach out, but Maria's focus stayed on her relationship. When the initial excitement of the relationship faded, Maria began to realize what she had lost. She started reaching out to her friends again, but it wasn't as easy as flipping a switch. Holly and the others were there for her, but the dynamic had shifted, and it took time to rebuild the closeness they once had.

The experience taught Maria a valuable lesson: That friendships aren't light switches you can turn on and off whenever it suits you. Relationships may change your priorities, but true friendships need nurturing, even when love is in the air.

Friends, Love & Making Time for Both

- **Love May Be in the Air, but Friendship Is on the Calendar:** If your friend is deep into the whirlwind of romance, it's your mission to sprinkle some friendship magic back into her life! Suggest a monthly movie night or a raucous college basketball game to keep the good times rolling. Try saying, "Let's declare the first Saturday of every month as our official catch-up day—bubbles and shenanigans included!" To keep the vibe light and breezy, propose some chill hangouts like a picnic in the park or a leisurely stroll together. Focus on mixing fun with connection and ensuring that you both have time to recharge your friendship batteries!

- **Just a Little "Miss Ya!":** If you are the one wrapped up in romance keep the connection open, a simple text like, "Miss you, let's catch up soon!" shows that your friends are still on your radar.

- **Keep It Light & Flexible:** If your friend seems caught up in their new love story, gently remind them you're still around with a playful touch. Say something like, "I'm thrilled for your love story, but let's not forget our weekly coffee catchups—I promise I won't third- wheel too hard!" While they're wrapped up in intimate dinners and love songs, let them know you're here whenever they need a break from all that sweetness. You could say, "I get it—you're balancing love, life, and stargazing. But hey, I'm here whenever you need a break from all that romance!" This approach keeps the mood light while reinforcing that your friendship still matters.

- **Ditch the Guilt Trip, Focus on the Fun:** Instead of guilt-tripping them, express how much you miss hanging out. "I miss our hangouts. Let's squeeze in some bestie time before you start finishing each other's sentences!" Schedule a wine tasting, attend a music festival, or have a casual BBQ where your friend can bring their new partner. This lets you all bond without anyone feeling left out.

As you wade through the romantic waters, don't let your friendships float away! Keep the laughter rolling and the hangouts coming, because the best relationships—platonic and romantic—include balance and a little bit of whimsy.

BEDROOM BANTER
How Much Do You Share?

Real talk: Are you and your bestie swapping bedroom stories, or is that diary sealed up tighter than a pair of skinny jeans after Thanksgiving dinner? Some of us are out here giving play-by-plays that would make a sports commentator blush, while others are more *what happens in the bedroom stays in the bedroom*. Me? I say spill the tea! There's something both hilarious and oddly educational about sharing the wild, awkward, and downright embarrassing moments. It's basically free entertainment! Who else is going to laugh with you about that moment when the mood music switched from Marvin Gaye to an ad for hemorrhoid cream? Of course, in the world of friendship, make sure you are both on the same page. No one wants to accidentally turn an afternoon hike into a confession they can't un-hear. So read the room, respect the boundaries, and if in doubt, ask before you unleash the juicy details!

Is Your Bestie Ready for TMI?
Not everyone's ready for a deep dive into your bedroom adventures, and that's totally cool. Before you start dishing out the steamy details, it's important to check if your bestie is in the mood for the X-rated version of events. Some friends are like, *Give me all the tea!* while others might want to keep things PG-13. A quick, "Hey, you ready for some TMI?" or "Mind if I share something a little spicy?" goes a long way. Think of it like getting a hall pass for the juicy stuff—consent before content, people! It saves you from turning a casual convo into an accidental *overshare* moment.

Humor Lightens the Mood, but Keep It Respectful
When it comes to bedroom banter, nothing breaks the ice quite like a well-timed joke. Sharing a funny mishap or clumsy moment can lead to the kind of belly laughs that remind us that: Sex doesn't *have* to be serious! But let's keep it classy, folks—while it's great to laugh about that time the bedsheet situation got out of control, we have also got to respect our partner's privacy. Just because you are telling *your* story doesn't mean you need to give a comprehensive overview of *someone else's* intimate life. Your friend doesn't need *all* the details, right?

Sex Talk = Support System

Talking about sex with your bestie isn't just about cracking jokes or spilling the latest bedroom drama. Sometimes, it's about being there when they need advice or a little pep talk. Maybe your friend's trying something new, dealing with a delicate situation (who hasn't?), or navigating relationship speed bumps. Having these open, judgment-free conversations can make all the difference. There's something pretty special about knowing you have got a front-row seat to the unpredictable path of life, passion, and all those *what just happened?* moments.

Know When to Dial It Back

Not every conversation needs to sound like a *Sex and the City* episode. If the topic starts to feel a little too heavy or like you are crossing into too-close-for comfort detail, it's totally okay to pump the brakes. Every friendship has its own rhythm—sometimes you are diving into steamy details, and other times you are just sharing the latest binge-worthy TV show (because balance is key!). The goal here is to keep the convo fun and supportive without it feeling like a never-ending sex-ed class.

Talking without the Taboos

At the heart of all this bedroom banter is something deeper—vulnerability. Talking about sex can bring up insecurities, questions, and downright confusing moments. Having these talks with a trusted friend is a safe way to explore those feelings, insecurities, and *yes,* even the uncomfortable ones. It's not just about dishing out details—it's about creating a space where you can be your truest, most raw self, knowing your friend is right there, no judgment.

Sip, Share & Squirm

One afternoon, while we were sipping coffee on my couch, my friend started opening up about some concerns she was having in the bedroom with her partner. It wasn't our usual conversation topic, but there we were—diving into the world of bedroom dilemmas. She hesitated at first, and I could tell she was debating how much to share. With a smirk, she finally broke the ice, saying, "Okay, don't laugh, but we've been having... let's call it 'technical difficulties.'"

I tried to hold back a chuckle, but let's be real—I was already bracing for the bizarre humor we were about to dive into. She went on to explain the comical moments, like when the mood lighting went from *romantic* to "I'm being interrogated by the FBI" because the dimmer switch broke. "And that one time, we were right in the middle of things when my dog decided to start barking at the vacuum cleaner in the corner. Talk about a mood killer!"

We both lost it laughing, and I reassured her that everyone's had those cringe-worthy moments. I reminded her that bedroom talk doesn't always have to be serious, and sometimes, you've just got to laugh your way through the awkwardness. I shared a story about when things got so chaotic for me that I accidentally kicked the nightstand while trying to be "graceful". It was not *graceful*.

As we kept talking, it turned into a mix of laughter an open dialogue. We found that blending humor with vulnerability made it easier to discuss the more serious stuff. It wasn't just about the silly mishaps anymore; it was about allowing freedom for her to talk about her feelings without judgment or embarrassment. I told her, "Hey, if it's not perfect every time, welcome to the club. The bloopers are part of the fun."

In the end, we had this unspoken agreement: We could laugh about the peculiar stuff, but we were also there for each other when things got serious. It became clear that bedroom banter, when shared with the right friend, isn't just about lighthearted chatter—it's about feeling safe enough to talk about real, sometimes uncomfortable parts of life. And let's face it, having someone to laugh with when the dog randomly decides to chase its tail in the middle of everything is priceless.

Spicing It Up While Keeping It Cool

- **Read the Room & Respect Boundaries:** If your friend starts checking their watch or changing the topic faster than a TV remote during commercials, take the hint! This is a cue to shift gears. Not everyone is always up for an in-depth chat, and that's okay. Also remember when you share those fun highlights leave out the overly personal details.

- **Keep It Light:** Humor is your friend here—say something like, "I had the funniest thing happen last night—you're going to lose it!" but keep the tone respectful. No need to drag other people's intimate details into the punchline.

- **No Judgy Vibes, Just Real Talk:** When your friend spills the details, skip the Judge Judy routine and focus on support. A simple, "I get how that could be tricky—here's what helped me," reassures them without making it feel like a courtroom. Let them know they can be vulnerable and offer a bit of your own story if it helps: "Honestly, I've felt that way too—it's more common than you think." The goal is to keep it light and let them know they're not alone.

- **Ask What They Need:** Before you bust out your pearls of wisdom, check in: "Do you want advice or just a sounding board?" Sometimes, they just need to vent without you turning into Dr. Phil.

- **Check the Vibe:** If things get a little too intense, smoothly transition with a lighthearted change. Say something like, "Alright, let's leave that topic on the nightstand—what's else is happening in your universe?" to keep the vibe chill.

- **Keep the Good Times Rolling:** Make sure your friend is still on board with the conversation. A simple, "Is this too much, or are we good?" can be all it takes to keep the balance.

As you dive into the world of bedroom banter, remember that these conversations can be a blend of laughter and vulnerability. Whether you're swapping tales of triumphs and hiccups or simply sharing a knowing look after a hilarious mishap, know that these moments create lasting connections. Keep the lines of communication open, add in some laughter, and embrace the messiness of it all!

33

GO WITH THE FLOW
The Art of Adaptability in Friendships

Just as the seasons change, so do our friendships, transforming and evolving as we experience life's many shifts and surprises. One minute, you're texting each other nonstop, planning to check out the next local event and swapping stories of every precious moment. The next thing you know, someone's moving across the country, diving headfirst into a new job, or juggling life's latest shake up—and suddenly, the *OMG, guess what happened* texts are fewer and farther between. Remember change doesn't mean the end of a friendship. It just means it's time to spread your adaptability wings and go with the flow. Think of it as your friendship's makeover moment.

Life Happens, and Friendships Can, Too

There will always be speed bumps on the road of friendship—like when your BFF's life transforms them into an around-the-clock-toddler-wrangler or when your workload turns your to-do list into a novel longer than the latest bestseller. Life can get messy, chaotic, and downright unpredictable. Maybe one of you gets a promotion that requires more hours, while the other starts juggling home improvement projects. Just because *Taco Tuesday* is on pause doesn't mean the connection has to fade. Instead, think of it as an opportunity to innovate how you spend time together. Once again, it's about prioritizing *quality* over *quantity*, finding joy in the little moments, and being flexible enough to adapt.

It's about the long game. Take it in stride and adapt to the changes life throws our way. Sometimes, you'll be glued to your phones all day, swapping memes and catching up, while other times, you might not talk for a week because one of you is knee-deep in deadlines or maneuvering the school drop-off line. And that's perfectly okay! Why not explore new ways to keep the friendship alive without stressing over the shifts?

Bend, Don't Break

Being adaptable is like becoming the yoga instructor of your friendship—go with the flow! Just as yoga teaches us to stretch and find balance, flexibility in friendships allows us to tackle life's hurdles without losing sight of what matters most.

Your friend might have moved into a new place and is in an unpacking frenzy, or you might have a month where everything feels chaotic, with birthdays, events, and life responsibilities piling up. Instead of feeling frustrated or distant, embrace the opportunity to get creative. You might find that impromptu video chats during lunch breaks become your new norm or that sending inspirational quotes turns into a delightful ritual. Explore these fresh avenues for connection and you will ensure that your friendship remains vibrant and fulfilling.

The intrigue of flexibility lies in the element of surprise. Who knew that voice memos while grocery shopping could become your new thing? Imagine sending your friend a quick audio clip while you're in the produce aisle, debating between apples and oranges. It's these spontaneous moments that add a new spin to your routine and keep the friendship dynamic.

Stretching Together: The Evolution of Friendship
Much like your favorite playlist, friendships *will* evolve and change over time, adapting to the different rhythms and beats of life. Just as you might shuffle songs to match your mood, your friendships should flex and adjust as you experience life's highs and lows, creating a harmonious blend of support and understanding. Whether it's celebrating a friend's new business opportunity, mourning a loss together, or sharing the excitement of embarking on new adventures, adaptability means recognizing that you both are evolving. By honoring the changes, you foster an environment for each person to grow individually. The more you embrace these changes, the stronger the bond becomes, transforming every bump in the road into an adventure you tackle together.

Traversing life's milestones, like going back to school or caring for an elderly parent, can sometimes feel overwhelming. However, these changes can also serve as opportunities to deepen your friendship. For instance, when a friend is juggling classes and assignments, they may not have much time for spontaneous outings. This is where adaptability shines: suggest casual get-togethers like study breaks over coffee or virtual hangouts where you can help them stay motivated.

Similarly, if your friend is stepping into the role of caregiver for an elderly parent, they might be adjusting their schedules significantly. In this case, offer to drop by with dinner or set up a movie night at their place, allowing them to take a breather while feeling supported. These moments of connection, tailored to new realities, keep your friendship alive and thriving, reminding both of you that change can bring you even closer.

Flexibility Over Frustration: Creating New Traditions

Andrea and her friend had been through peaks and valleys, inner circle besties—wild party nights in their twenties, and now managing household chaos in their thirties. Their Sunday morning hikes had become a sacred tradition, a time to unwind from busy weeks and endless kids' activities. But life has a funny way of changing routines, Andrea's friend found herself embracing something new—her church community. Sunday mornings were no longer about hikes but about attending services, and this sudden shift left Andrea feeling a little lost.

At first, Andrea struggled with the change. She missed their regular catchups and the fresh air they enjoyed together. Instead of letting this change build resentment or come between them, she leaned into adaptability. She knew her friend was genuinely excited about this new chapter in her life, so Andrea chose to be supportive rather than frustrated. With a bit of creativity and compromise, they decided to move their weekly hikes to early Friday mornings, catching the sunrise before the chaos of the day set in.

This small shift turned out to be a blessing in disguise. Not only did Andrea get to continue their cherished tradition, but the peacefulness of the early morning hikes brought a new energy to their friendship. They created fresh memories—laughing about how hard it was to wake up that early, but grateful for the quiet moments they shared before their busy lives took over. Andrea realized that when life changes, the best way to keep friendships alive is to adapt and find new rhythms.

The Friendship Adjustment Bureau

- **Set New Norms:** When life feels like a whirlwind, it's time to recalibrate your expectations. Lighten the mood with a playful check in, like, "Hey, I know life's doing backflips for you right now—how can we keep the friendship spark alive without cramming our schedules with fleeting catchups?"

- **Embrace New Formats:** If in-person hangouts are off the table, don't fret! Try this instead: "How about we swap quick voice notes during the week? It's like chatting, but without the pressure of matching our calendars!"

- **Plan Mini Check Ins:** Sometimes life doesn't give you an hour to chat, but it can give you 10 minutes. Schedule low-pressure check ins like a mini FaceTime during lunch or a simple *thinking of you* text. It keeps the bond strong without stress.

- **Adjust Together:** Big changes on the horizon? No sweat. Have a casual touch base: "Hey, life's shifting—how can I support you and make sure our friendship stays as fantastic as ever?"

- **Practice Patience with Change:** When the vibes feel off, drop your friend a line like, "I know life's a bit chaotic right now, but I'm here for you. Let's figure out our new groove together—preferably one that involves *queso!*"

- **Reassess and Adjust:** Every so often, hit the refresh button. Ask your friend, "Hey, how are we doing? Should we tweak our hangout strategy to discuss life's latest developments?"

Adaptability is like a game of Tetris—sometimes you perfectly slot the pieces in, and other times you're just trying to keep everything from toppling over into a colorful chaos. Keep stacking those memories like you are competing for that high score, stay adaptable and don't sweat it when life is so crazy that you accidentally send your friend a selfie of your cat looking more fabulous than your lunch. Remember, those little blunders are just bonus rounds in the friendship journey!

REBUILDING BRIDGES
How to Reconnect with Friends after Time Apart

Maybe you have let a friendship drift for a while, and now you're wondering how to reconnect without it feeling like those dreadful high school reunions. No sweat! Think of it like picking up a book you put down ages ago—the story's still there, you just need to dive back in.

Break the Ice
You know those icebreakers that make you want to run for the hills? Yeah, skip those. Instead, start with something casual and lighthearted. "Hey! It feels like ages since we last talked—what's new in your world?" works wonders. It's like slipping into a comfy pair of old shoes—no need for anything fancy, just genuine curiosity. And, humor always helps: "I think I owe you about 20 life updates... Wanna grab a coffee and compare notes?"

Reconnect without Regret
Life happens, and we have all ghosted a friend or two (unintentionally, of course). But there's no need to bring a suitcase of guilt to the reunion. You don't need to explain every missed call or text like you're presenting evidence in court. A simple, "It's been a minute, but I've missed you," is enough. The goal here is to focus on moving forward, not replaying why you lost touch in the first place.

Share the Laughs, Even the Embarrassing Ones
Remember when you both got lost trying to find that party, or the time you accidentally walked into a random wedding instead of your friend's birthday bash? Tap into those golden memories. Shared laughter is the easiest way to bridge any gap—plus, it reminds you both why the friendship mattered in the first place. Throw in a "Remember that time we went to that costume party, but it wasn't really a costume party and there we were in our Mickey and Minnie outfits?" and watch the tension melt away.

Make It Easy to Hang Out
Reconnecting doesn't have to be an epic adventure. Sure, planning a

trip to Italy sounds great, but it's the simple stuff that makes rebuilding friendships easy. Suggest a laid-back hangout, like hitting up a local farmer's market, going for a hike, or having a night playing cards. You could even do something sentimental, like flipping through old photos or trying to recreate that delicious Moscow mule you both loved. If you really want to make it fun, throw in something totally unexpected, like, "Let's meet up and see who can still do a cartwheel without pulling a muscle!"

Let It Flow
Don't stress if things feel a little different at first—that's normal. You're both catching up, maybe with some new eccentricities or habits thrown in. Roll with it! Focus on creating new memories, even if it means you're now bonding over slightly more adult activities (hello, mortgage talk). Just remember, there's no need to recreate the past—it's all about where you're heading now.

Resist the urge to overthink it. You don't need a friendship strategy with bullet points (though, hey, I won't judge). Some friendships pick up exactly where they left off, others take a bit more nurturing. Go at your own pace. Whether it's grabbing a quick bite at a local food truck, catching up over a leisurely walk in the park, or even joining a fun class together (like pottery or dance), the key is showing up and being authentic. Your friend will appreciate the effort, and the rest will fall into place.

From a Simple Text to a Warm Welcome
When I made my move to Arizona, I knew a couple of people but hadn't stayed close with them over the years. Two friends from my old hometown had also relocated here years prior, and a high school friend I hadn't seen in forever was living nearby. After months of preparing for the move, I sent a simple message, "Hey, I miss you guys, and I'll be your neighbor soon!" I didn't expect much, but the response was heartwarming and immediate.

The morning after I arrived, my high school friend knocked on my door, not with just words of encouragement but with her husband, coffee, donuts and the willingness to help me unpack. We hadn't seen each other in years, yet she showed up without hesitation. It was like no time had passed at all. My two hometown friends, whom I hadn't connected with much since they'd moved, immediately reached out as well, inviting me to everything from local festivals to backyard get-togethers.

Those small gestures quickly transformed into the rekindling of deep friendships. The years of distance didn't matter. All it took was a little nudge and a single text to break the ice. These old friends helped me settle into my new life in Arizona and made it feel like home. What could have been an isolating time became one of warmth, laughter, and reconnection.

The charm of these friendships reminded me that sometimes, all it takes is the courage to reach out and let the rest unfold naturally. Those bridges weren't as far gone as I had thought, and I'm so grateful I took the chance to rebuild them.

Simple Moves to Reignite the Bond

- **Send a Lighthearted Message:** Start with something simple and warm like, "I've been thinking about you! Let's catch up soon."

- **Tap Into Humor:** Bring up a funny memory to break the ice and remind you both of the good times.

- **Plan a Casual Hangout:** Suggest easy, low-pressure activities like a coffee date or a walk—no need for anything elaborate.

- **Embrace Change:** Don't try to force the friendship back to how it was. Focus on creating new, fun memories together.

Reconnecting with friends after time apart is like dusting off an old record. At first, it may feel a bit scratchy, but once it spins back into the groove, the familiar tunes bring back all the good vibes. Just remember you can pick up right where you left off, it just takes a little courage to reach out and a willingness to embrace the rhythm of your evolving lives. Here's to rekindling those connections and making beautiful music together again!

35

THE ROOMMATE REMIX
Friendship Meets Shared Spaces

Living with your best friend sounds like a dream come true, right? Endless movie nights, sharing clothes, and always having someone to laugh with. HOWEVER—when you are sharing the same space 24/7, reality has a funny way of showing up, and things can get a little *too* real. Even the best friendships can hit bumps when personal habits, idiosyncrasies, and boundaries are tested. And no, it's not just about who's leaving the toilet seat up.

How do you keep your friendship thriving while living under the same roof? The essentials—Balance, communication, and a touch of compromise (okay, a LOT of compromise). Hold onto your hats; this friendship adventure is about to take off!

Space Is Key (Even When It's Tight!)

No matter how much you love hanging out, everyone needs their personal space. Living with a friend doesn't mean you have to spend *every* moment together. It's important to carve out time for yourself, whether it's taking a solo walk, reading in your room, or having a quiet coffee break. Respecting each other's alone time is key to keeping things smooth. You don't necessarily have to schedule it but knowing when to give each other space is a lifesaver.

Communicate the Little Things Before They Get Big!

Everyone has their little quirks—whether it's leaving dishes in the sink, blasting music at 7am, or hoarding all the good snacks. The key here? Communicate before these tiny annoyances become full-blown roommate rants. If your friend's habit of leaving peanut butter knives on the counter is driving you nuts, casually bring it up before you snap: "Love you, but can the peanut butter knives not become a kitchen sculpture?"

Set Boundaries Early & Stick to Them!

You're living together, not morphing into the same person. It's totally okay to say, "I need quiet time after work," or "Let's do a deep clean every Saturday." If you set boundaries early, you can avoid passive-aggressive sticky notes later (and trust me, *no one* likes those).

Think about all the little things that matter to you, even if they seem minor. If you need a clutter-free kitchen to unwind, say it upfront. Or if you have specific sleep and wake times, make those known.

Don't forget to be open to their needs, too. Check in periodically to make sure the ground rules still work for both of you; life changes, and sometimes routines do, too. These aren't set in stone—they're more like guidelines that help you create a comfortable and respectful environment. Be ready to revisit them if things start feeling tense or out of sync. Having these conversations early on isn't about control; it's about making sure you both feel comfortable and respected in your shared space.

The Art of Compromise
Ah, compromise. The backbone of every successful roommate situation. Maybe they love hosting friends, and you enjoy a quiet space. Or maybe they keep the apartment at Antarctic temperatures while you are wrapped in five blankets. Meeting in the middle is the key to survival. Just think of it as a roommate dance—sometimes you lead, sometimes you follow, and occasionally you step on each other's toes. But hey, with a little rhythm, you will find your groove and keep things moving smoothly.

Have Fun with It
Don't forget, the real joy of living with your friend is the fun you get to have! Whether it's trying new recipes (and maybe burning them), hosting themed movie nights, or tackling a DIY project, remember to enjoy the experience. You are living together because you like each other, so lean into that and make memories (just preferably ones that don't involve accidentally flooding the bathroom).

When It's Time for a Friend-cation
Yes, sometimes living with a friend can feel like a bit much (shocker!). If things start feeling tense, it's okay to take a breather. A weekend apart or a solo adventure might be just what you both need to renew your spirits and keep things light.

Whitney & the Dish Rag Saga

My friend Whitney was telling me this cute story about her college days when she had an OCD moment with her roommate. Whitney's roommate was fantastic about keeping the kitchen spotless, doing the dishes, and tidying up after meals. But there was one habit that absolutely drove Whitney up the wall—how her roommate handled the wet dish rag after cleaning. Instead of hanging it to dry, her roommate would bunch it up and toss it into the corner of the sink, leaving it to fester and, eventually, stink like mildew.

Whitney tried to let it go, but each time she encountered that wet, musty rag, it slowly ate at her tolerance. Finally, after one too many smelly encounters, Whitney had to have a chat with her roommate and was worried about bringing it up, but to Whitney's relief, her roommate didn't take it personally at all. In fact, she laughed it off and welcomed Whitney's advice on how to properly dry and fold the rag to prevent the mildew smell.

What made the story even better is that years later Whitney ran into her old roommate, and guess what? She still uses Whitney's rag-folding method! Her roommate thanked her for the tip, admitting it had become part of her daily routine ever since. It's funny how even the smallest habits can stick around, and how something as simple as a smelly rag turned into a memory that lasted a lifetime.

What could've become a source of frustration was quickly solved with a friendly conversation, bringing Whitney and her roommate closer in the process. Whether it's a soggy dish rag or clashing cleaning habits, it's the communication and mutual respect that keep things running smoothly and help friendships stay solid, even in the shared spaces of daily life.

Roommate Harmony: Balancing Fun & Space

- **Ground Rules & Good Vibes:** Before issues arise, discuss habits and preferences. During your first week, talk about things like sleep schedules, noise levels, and cleaning. For example, "I'm a night owl—are there certain times you'd like to keep the noise down?" Or "Let's keep mornings chill with no talking until coffee's been consumed."

- **Harmony Hack:** Establish a cleaning schedule that works for both of you to avoid any "Wait, I cleaned last week!" moments. Identify areas where compromise is needed (like that temperature battle) and find middle ground. "Okay, you can keep it freezing in the living room, but I get the bedroom heater." Test compromises for a week and adjust as needed. Say, "Let's try this for a bit and see if we need to tweak anything."

- **Touch-Base Tuesdays:** Set aside time for quick weekly check ins, where you both can say, "What's working and what's... not?"

- **Recharge on Your Own Terms:** Everyone needs personal time, so give each other a heads-up. "I'm diving into my podcast solo tonight, so let's catch up tomorrow!" Acknowledge when tension's brewing by planning solo activities or even short trips apart. "I'm heading out for a solo road trip this weekend—let's catch up when I get back."

- **Roomie Rituals:** Establish small traditions, like Saturday pancakes or Friday karaoke night. It's the little things that keep the bond strong. And think about setting aside time to just be silly and have fun together— whether it's a crafting frenzy, spontaneous road trip, or "let's try every weird activity on Groupon" adventure, the important thing is that you're making memories.

- **Laugh It Off:** When challenges arise, remind yourself why you chose to live together. Take a moment to laugh about it then hit that reset button.

Living with your bestie is like the ultimate slumber party that never ends. Sure, you'll have a few epic clashes over cleaning and personal space (hello, thermostat wars), but you'll also build memories that last way beyond the lease. Here's to surviving soggy dish rags, dance parties in the living room, and finding the right balance of love, space, and a healthy dose of laughter. After all, the goal is to have fun together—not just survive as roomies!

CUBICLE CHRONICLES
Juggling BFFs and Business in the Workplace

Workplace friends are a whole different breed of amazing. These are the people who know exactly when you need that 3pm caffeine fix or when you are on the verge of losing it over that one coworker who *always* replies all. Whether it's the inside jokes that no one else gets, the shared eye rolls during those never-ending Zoom meetings, or the sly texts during boring presentations, work besties make the office grind not only bearable but sometimes downright fun. Still...as much as we love gossiping over coffee, navigating the delicate line between professional and personal can sometimes feel like dodging landmines.

The Perks of Having a Work Bestie

Having a workplace friend is a total game-changer. They are your personal cheerleader, partner in crime, and venting buddy all rolled into one. Need someone to laugh about the quirky office decor? Got a mid-morning craving for donuts but don't want to go alone? Your work bestie's got your back. Plus, they totally get that *one email* that can turn your day upside down. They are your daily dose of sanity.

Besties in Business: The Art of Staying Professional

As great as your work bestie is, you've still got to navigate that delicate balance between friend and colleague. While it's fun to talk about everything, from your weekend plans to that annoying person in accounting, don't let your friendship derail your professionalism. Ya gotta find that sweet spot—where you can laugh at the absurdity of office life but still get stuff done without turning the workplace into your own personal reality show.

Navigating Office Politics

Office politics can be a tricky maze. One minute, you and your work bestie are talking smack about the same person, and the next minute, one of you might need to work with them closely. It's easy to fall into the *us vs. them* trap, but if you want to keep your friendships—and your sanity—intact, it's important to steer clear of gossiping about colleagues. Remember, you are in this together for the long haul, not a season of *The Office: Drama Edition*.

From Colleague to Confidant Without Crossing the Line

Turning a coworker into a close friend takes finesse. Sure, you bond over mutual hatred of 4pm Friday meetings but transitioning that into a genuine friendship takes some work. Start with those casual after-work hangouts—just be sure to keep it professional during office hours, or you might drift into murky territory. If your coffee break is starting to sound more like a therapy session, it might be time to take that conversation outside the office.

Keeping It Chill When Roles Shift

Sometimes the office dynamic changes. Maybe your office sidekick gets promoted, and now they are your boss, or maybe they switch departments. Things may start to feel different. Give yourselves permission to step back when needed, reevaluate boundaries, and figure out how the new dynamic can work without things feeling strained. After all, it's hard to grab drinks when your friend just gave you a 30-minute constructive feedback session.

Your Next Bestie Could Be on the Other Side of That Zoom Call

Friendships have a funny way of sneaking up on you, especially in places you least expect—like a Zoom call. One of my friends was sharing with me the story of a work meeting she had years ago with a colleague. After the call, my friend felt compelled to offer some honest feedback to her office mate. She kindly let her know that her tone throughout the meeting wasn't exactly warm or approachable and had made a few people uncomfortable. At first, the woman was shocked—who wouldn't be? But instead of brushing it off, she took the feedback to heart.

The real heart of this story is that colleague took the feedback and adjusted her tone going forward without compromising her authenticity. The small change she made helped shift her professional demeanor, and over time, this moment of candid feedback blossomed into a friendship that has now lasted over 20 years.

Sometimes, the person you least expect could become your closest friend. All it takes is a bit of honesty, mutual growth, and an openness to seeing beyond that initial impression. Whether it's a Zoom meeting or a chat by the water cooler, friendships can emerge from the most unexpected encounters.

So, the next time you're in a virtual meeting, keep an open mind—you never know, your future bestie could be just one honest conversation away!

Office Besties 101: Balancing Fun & Focus

- **Boost Each Other Up with Laughs & Encouragement:** A quick "We're almost there!" or sharing office jokes only the two of you will get helps keep the mood light and boosts morale through stressful days. It's like a secret language that keeps you both laughing through the daily challenges.

- **The Friendly Work Pause:** During work hours keep your chats light and save the serious talks for when you are not on the clock. If your friend's story about their wild weekend starts to take over your workday, don't hesitate to say, "How about we keep the juicy details for happy hour! Love our chats, but maybe we dive into the deep stuff after 5pm?" It keeps things light and focused, ensuring you both enjoy the moment without losing track of your day.

- **Support, Don't Roast:** When your work bestie wants to vent about another coworker, steer the conversation toward solutions. Try saying, "Yeah, that's rough, now how can we fix it?" If the conversation turns into a full-blown roast of someone else, redirect it with humor: "Let's focus on surviving this project first—then we can dish."

- **Make It Social Beyond the Cubicle:** Organize after-work hangouts to deepen the friendship beyond the office. Suggest, "Let's grab lunch this weekend and catch up outside of work!"

- **Laugh through the Role Swap:** If your friend becomes your boss, say, "So, drinks after work—boss's treat, right?" And acknowledge the change, "Things are changing, but we've got this! Let's keep our personal and professional lives balanced."

- **Constructive Cheers:** Instead of just celebrating wins, make it a habit to offer constructive feedback in a supportive way. Say something like, "You did great on that presentation—next time, we should tackle the Q&A together, I have some ideas on how to get people more involved!"

- **Beyond the Office Badge—Keeping Friendships Strong:** Even if you or your work bestie move to a new job, make that effort to stay connected through regular check ins or occasional catch-up dinners.

Cubical companions are the unsung heroes of the office world. They make the dull moments brighter, the tough days survivable, and the long hours a little less miserable. And when nurtured properly, these friendships don't just fizzle out when someone changes jobs—they last. When work gets chaotic, remember to laugh, (I know I keep telling you to laugh) vent appropriately, and support each other through the grind. You are not just coworkers—they are your teammates

🦩🦩 Together We Thrive

When I got divorced, I had a moment of pure panic—like, "Wait, who's going to check in on me now? Who's my emergency contact? If I go on a date and never come back, who's going to track me down like a true crime podcast episode?" Enter my friends, capes and all. They didn't miss a beat. Suddenly, we were sharing locations like we were on some covert mission, checking in after dates like I had just entered *The Hunger Games* of romance, and my gals even became my occasional private investigator. It's wild how those practical things—like making sure I didn't disappear into the void—became acts of love. That's the thing about genuine friends—they find new ways to support you, they meet every twist and turn with you head-on, and stick by your side through whatever life hurls in your direction. In my case, they didn't just have my back; they became my new life support system, emergency contact, and, yes, sometimes my own version of 911 on speed dial.

As life has shifted, so have the roles we play in each other's lives—like trading superpowers depending on the day. One of the things I treasure most is how my friendships lift me up, sometimes quite literally (hello, emotional support on those *I-can't-adult-today* days). I'm surrounded by these incredible, talented women who push me to grow—and not in a subtle way, more like, "You got this, now get moving!" They've walked me through the roller-coaster of starting my own business—complete with the loops and dips, and in return I've helped some of them craft their LinkedIn profiles and resumes (aka professional hype-woman duty).

Together, we're like a powerhouse squad, and our network stretches far beyond just a wine night. We're always on the lookout for ways to help each other level up—whether it's sharing resources, cooking up new concepts, or just sending a well-timed "You're unstoppable" text.

Perhaps the most inspiring aspect? A tribe isn't just about personal growth; we can unite them to drive positive change in our communities. Imagine the impact we can create when we harness our collective strengths for a cause we all believe in! Whether it's organizing a fundraiser, volunteering for a local charity, or rallying to advocate for change, our friendships become a catalyst for something greater. It's incredible to witness how each individual brings unique skills to the table, transforming our connections into a movement for good. Honestly? I know I could be tapping into this even more because my tribe has the kind of potential that could shake things up in epic, world-changing ways! But in a totally supportive, non-villainous way, of course.

To take it a step further, celebrating our differences means diving into each other's backgrounds, values, and life experiences on a deeper level. It's one thing to laugh over fashion choices and weekend plans, but real connection comes from understanding the journey that got each of us here—the beliefs, challenges, and victories that shape how we see the world. We don't always have to agree (thank goodness, right?), but taking a peek from their side of the fence can be a game-changer.

Whitney grew up in a bustling city that, shaped her bold energy and quick-witted humor, while Charlotte's small-town roots mean she's more reserved and steady as a rock when you need her. It's not just about geography, though; it's also about the layers underneath, the stories that can make us laugh, cry, or rethink our perspectives. And then there is the unique entertainment they bring. Whitney might drag me to a drag show (yes, please!) while Charlotte is revving up for actual drag races (I'll bring earplugs!). And guess what? I'm down for both! By exploring these layers, we give each other the respect and trust to feel safe, knowing that personalities, beliefs, and histories are all valued in our own unique ways.

While we nudge one another to try new things, let's talk about a whole different kind of push—friendly competition, the kind that's equal parts motivating and mildly infuriating. I have one friend who's always roping me into healthy challenges. "Let's sync our Apple watches and close all the activity circles!" she'll say with all the enthusiasm of a fitness guru. Does it drive me a little batty sometimes? Absolutely, especially on days like today, when I've been sitting at my desk writing for nine hours straight and haven't closed a single circle. Is there a sitting marathon I missed out on? In the end, I love it! It's a fun connection that keeps us both motivated, even when my activity tracker looks more like a nap schedule. Healthy competition between friends isn't about winning or losing—it's that little spark that pushes us to be better, while also giving us plenty of opportunities to tease each other along the way.

And now we're at the final section of the book, where we celebrate those transformative friendships—the ones that aren't just checking in, the ones that are truly showing up. Whether we're helping each other rise up, embracing our wildly different personalities, or engaging in a bit of playful rivalry, these are the relationships that make life so much richer, and together, we thrive!

EMERGENCY CONTACT ENERGY
Next-Level Friendship Care

TRUE friendship care goes beyond the usual check ins and true-to-life conversations. We're talking about stepping into some unexpected (and hilariously important) roles, like being their emergency contact (because, seriously, who even has one?). Caring for your friends means being the one they can count on—from braving a first date to figuring out how to create a spreadsheet without breaking into a sweat.

Be the Ultimate Emergency Contact

You know you've reached peak friendship status when, faced with the question "Who is your emergency contact?" they confidently write down your name. It's more than just a box on a form—it's the assurance that, if they ever face a real emergency, you're the person they want to be called. Whether it's a medical situation, an unexpected crisis, or just the peace of knowing someone's in their corner, you're their reliable lifeline.

First-Date Safety Patrol & Everything Inbetween

Nothing says *I've got your back* like being the behind-the-scenes bodyguard during a first date. Forget the usual *good luck* text; you're the friend making sure they share their location because, hey, it's the modern era, and safety first. Whether you are sending a *How's it going?* check in or the classic *Need a rescue?* text, you are the secret agent keeping your bestie grounded.

And it's not just dates—you're their lifeline when they're stranded at an airport at 3am, desperate for someone to help them find the nearest all-night coffee shop so they can stay awake until their rescheduled flight. You're their all-purpose lifesaver when they need a ride home after a night that started with 'just one drink" and turned into a full-on conga line. You're also the one they call when they're locked out of their apartment in pajamas with a carton of ice cream in hand, or when they realize they accidentally wandered into a retirement party and need a smooth exit.

It's the kind of care that's both practical and delightfully thoughtful— like a guardian angel with a cell phone, ready to swoop in with spare keys

197

or just the perfect *pretend I need you* call. Whatever the situation, you're there to keep things safe, light-hearted, and mostly drama-free.

Be Their Google Guide

Got a friend who has a full-blown panic attack trying to set up a budget or navigate tech? That's where you come in. You are their personal Google, but way cooler. Whether it's decoding a finance app or teaching them how to make a boomerang on Instagram you've got the answers. You jump in, because caring means being their first call for things that might be overwhelming for them but are a piece of cake for you.

Help with Life's To-Do List

You know that *life admin* stuff everyone loves to avoid? Sometimes being a caring friend is diving in to help with the mundane. Whether they're packing for a move or finally purging their pantry, you're there, sleeves rolled up, snacks in hand, ready to tackle it together. It's those little acts of care that make a big difference, and it shows that you are invested in their well-being.

Doctor's Appointment Duty

Now and then, friendship care means being their Uber driver and after care nurse, especially when your friend's facing something they've been dreading (hello, colonoscopy). You are the one calming their nerves, sitting in the waiting room, and offering post-appointment comfort food. Because, if you can't be there with a box of bagels, are you even a friend? Being that friend who's there when things get serious means more than words can say.

Emergency Contact Vibes: Friendship That's Got Your Back

When I moved to Arizona, I knew the transition wouldn't just be about unpacking boxes and finding a new grocery store—it also meant setting up care with a whole new group of doctors. Welcome to life at 50! Every new doctor meant piles of paperwork and the dreaded, *Who's your emergency contact?* question staring back at me. And the reality hit—my circle of close friends was a few states away. Yikes!

Luckily, I had those old hometown friends who weren't too far, including my dear friend Jodi. When I had a few medical procedures lined up and needed rides to and from appointments, I hesitated to ask anyone. It's no small thing to take time out of your day when you've got kids you are running to sports practices and your own life to manage. Without a second of hesitation, Jodi jumped right in. She was my personal chauffeur and support system all rolled into one.

Jodi made sure she had all the details—she got the location of the doctor's office, picked me up with time to spare, and got me there without a hitch. After the procedure, she was the first face I saw. She got me back home, and over the next 24 hours, she checked in on me multiple times to make sure I was recovering well. As a single woman making my way in a new town, having Jodi there for me in those moments was more than just a ride—it was a lifeline.

It's moments like these that remind you what true friendship care looks like. It goes beyond just checking in over text. It's stepping up when it really counts and offering the kind of support that fills in all the gaps. Knowing Jodi was there for me brought me a deep sense of comfort and connection, and I'm so grateful to have her on my emergency contact list—literally and figuratively!

Ready for Anything: How to Be the Ultimate Go-To Friend

- **Emergency Contact Extraordinaire:** Have a plan ready, complete with "In Case of Crisis" notes. Think of it as prepping for your friend's disaster movie moment (minus the special effects) while keeping them cozy and secure.

- **Big Day Buddy & Comfort Concierge:** Chat beforehand about their worries, whether it's medical or just the fear of waiting rooms. Offer to be their sidekick for the day, complete with entertainment and hydration essentials. If they need downtime afterward, offer to spend the evening with them or bring their favorite treat (or a questionable rom-com) to help them recover and feel loved.

- **Secret Signals & Drop a Pin:** Create a safe word (or emoji!) for discreet date escapes. A simple "I just saw the weirdest cat video" could be the signal to swoop in. Also, ask them to drop a pin on their location and then get ready to live out your own spy fantasy.

- **DIY How-To, with a Twist:** From budgeting to setting up their new smart TV, send easy, step-by-step guides. You can even throw in some humor: "Step 1: Breathe. Step 2: Don't panic."

- **Get-It-Done Buddy:** Check in on longer projects—like, "How's that budget disaster coming along?"—and help break big tasks into bite-sized chunks. Offer to do the first few steps with them, like when they are redecorating, help them choose paint colors or assemble furniture or if they are planning a big event, help them create a guest list and pick out decor—just don't let them procrastinate by watching *just one more episode!*

- **Accountability, Baby:** Send little reminders to keep them on track. Nothing says, "I care" like checking in with "Hey, did you survive step two of your to-do list?"

Showing up for your friends doesn't always mean elaborate efforts—it's about being there for the big stuff *and* the little things. From keeping them safe on a first date to figuring out life's tedious tasks, true friendship care is knowing they can count on you in any situation. So, stock up on casseroles, stay on standby, and remember you're their emergency contact for life (and maybe, if you're lucky, also their co-investigator on all alien conspiracy theories).

THE POWER OF THE COLLECTIVE
Uniting Your Tribe for Something Bigger

Ever notice how each of your friends brings something totally original to the table? One friend is the master of organizing chaotic group chats, while another is basically the walking encyclopedia of wisdom. They all come from different walks of life, with their own strengths, perspectives, and experiences. Now, imagine what could happen if you brought them all together for something bigger. That's the true power of the collective—taking those one-on-one friendships and blending them into a force that can create real change (or at least throw one epic dinner party).

Bringing your friends together doesn't have to be a serious 'let's change the world' meeting—at least not right away. It can start with something simple, like hosting a fun gathering where everyone meets and bonds over shared interests (or how bad the traffic was getting there). But beyond the laughs and inside jokes, there's an opportunity to collaborate in ways that make a difference, whether it's giving back to the community, starting a creative project, or even setting up informal mentorship circles. When friends from different backgrounds come together, the possibilities are endless. Seriously, you never know when someone's Excel skills (me, me, me) and another's bake sale expertise (not me, not me, not me) might combine to save the day!

When you unite your tribe, each person can bring their own unrivaled energy to the group. Maybe one friend is super passionate about environmental causes, another has a hidden talent of organizing *anything*, and yet another is great at rallying people to take action (aka, they have been hosting group adventures since 2009). When you combine those talents and passions, you have got the Avengers of friendship—ready to create something effective that none could have achieved solo.

Turn Friendship into Action
Once your friends are vibing and clicking like a perfectly synced dance crew, why not take it a step further? You can turn that energy into action, whether it's volunteering, starting a creative project, or planning a group trip with a purpose. Get your tribe involved in something meaningful

and watch something very powerful happen. Maybe you decide to host a fundraiser for a cause close to your hearts or put together care packages for those in need. Whatever you choose, it's about taking the bond you have and channeling it into something bigger than yourselves—kind of like when everyone brings the best drinks to a party, and suddenly it's the best party ever.

Mix & Mingle Masterclass
Nothing beats the vibe when your tribe comes together, each friend learning from the other and sparking inspiration left and right. There's something special about seeing friends from different walks of life build each other up, and make a bigger impact. You don't have to change the world overnight—this isn't a *Mission Impossible*—but when you blend your friendships into a collective, you create waves that flow far beyond your inner circle. Plus, you will probably pick up some new skills along the way, like mastering the timing of a graceful exit before cleanup duty starts.

From Event to Ritual
Once you have unleashed the power of your collective, don't let it fizzle out! Whether it's gathering essentials for food banks, organizing neighborhood recycling days, coordinating blood drives, or joining together for mindfulness challenges, turn these activities into annual or monthly traditions. What starts as a one-time event can become something you all look forward to and plan together regularly—like Friendsgiving, with more community benefit and fewer turkey disasters.

Walking for Hope: A Journey of Strength, Friendship & Love
About 20 years ago, when we still had a little more spring in our step, our dear friend's partner received the devastating news of a breast cancer diagnosis. In the midst of her overwhelming emotions, our friend was determined to channel her energy into something positive, something that would make an impact. She inspired six of us to participate in the Susan G. Komen 3-Day Walk for breast cancer—a challenging event that demanded physical stamina and mental strength, as we collectively raised funds and awareness for the fight against this heartbreaking disease.

The challenge was real—60 miles over three days, camping in tiny pink tents at night, and each of us had to raise $2,500 in donations. None of us hesitated. We rallied together, spreading the word to family, friends, and coworkers. The fundraiser required effort, and even more went into preparing our bodies for the grueling walk. We'd lace up our sneakers and spend our weekends walking miles at a time, trying to build the endurance we'd need. But it wasn't just about the training—it was about walking for a purpose. Each mile felt like a tribute to the women, who were battling breast cancer.

The weekend of the walk finally came, and we joined thousands of others, all with their own reasons for being there, all united in one common goal. The atmosphere was electric, with cheers and support lining the route. We walked mile after mile, through pain, blisters, and fatigue, but knowing what—and who—we were walking for kept us going. The nights were tough too, sleeping in those small tents with sore muscles, but the camaraderie we shared made the discomfort easier to bear.

By the third day, we were exhausted and determined. As we neared the finish line, we walked into the most beautiful stadium filled with cheering crowds, the energy uplifting us in our final steps. It was a moment of triumph, not just for completing the walk but for standing together in the fight against breast cancer. We gathered around our friend, hugging, crying, and reflecting on what we had accomplished. Her partner, who had been fighting so bravely, was waiting for us at the finish line, and seeing her made every blister, every mile, worth it. Sadly, her battle with cancer ended just a short time after the walk. We lost her, but the memory of that weekend lives on in all of us. It was more than just a walk—it was a way to stand beside our friend during one of the hardest times in her life. It was a reminder of the power of community, the importance of support, and the legacy of those we've loved and lost to this terrible disease.

Harnessing Your Tribe for a Bigger Purpose

- **Gather the Crew & Get Inspired:** Start small by organizing a casual gathering, like a night of bunco or sushi Saturday, where everyone can meet. Use conversation prompts or icebreakers to help people bond over common interests (or shared love of *queso* —ya, that's me again!).

- **Big Ideas, Bigger Impact:** At the gathering, explore shared interests or causes everyone feels passionate about. For example, ask, "If we all had a golden ticket for one day, how would we use it to do something good?"

- **Strengths United in the Ultimate Friend Project:** Use everyone's strengths to create a group project. If some friends love cooking, host a bake sale for charity. If others are into fitness, organize a charity run. And if someone's main talent is being a people-person, put them in charge of the pep talk. It doesn't have to be huge—small efforts can still have a big impact.

- **Team Up for a Cause:** Find a local cause you all care about and sign up for a volunteer day. Whether it's at an animal shelter, food bank, or environmental cleanup, these shared experiences are basically friendship fuel.

- **Meet, Give, Repeat:** Make group gatherings a regular thing. Whether it's monthly think tank sessions or yearly charity events, keeping things consistent helps maintain that team spirit and momentum.

- **Mark the Moment:** After tackling a major milestone, don't let the moment pass by. Plan a fun post-event hangout, give special shout-outs in your group chat, or start a shared Facebook album to capture all your collective wins. If you don't post about it, did it even happen?

Imagine the results when your group combines powers—not for world domination, but maybe for world improvement! You might not change the world overnight (no one expects you to design a new public transit system over lattes), but each act adds up. So keep plotting those small, mighty plans, and make every meet-up a force for good, because saving the world with your besties is next-level friendship.

SPICE IT UP
Celebrating the Magic of Our Differences!

The heart of our gatherings isn't only about showing up; it's about each person bringing something unique and wonderfully their own. Whether it's a friend's signature humor, another's passion for good causes, or a playlist that becomes the night's soundtrack, these little contributions make every get-together memorable. And what makes it even more powerful? The fact that we're all coming from different backgrounds, cultures, family traditions, and life experiences.

Regardless of where we come from, we're here to see each other as glorious individuals, celebrating life stories and deeper perspectives that make us who we are. Maybe it's a friend's deep-dish pizza loyalty in a room full of thin-crust fans, or their unexpected passion for debating economic issues that challenges you to look beyond your comfort zone. Perhaps it's a friend who grew up halfway across the world, bringing insights on community and family that make you rethink what 'connection' truly means, or the friend with an activist spirit, pushing you to see the bigger picture on issues like climate change and social justice.

These surprising differences create bonds that transcend small talk, sparking conversations that expand our horizons and remind us why diverse perspectives are invaluable. Life would be pretty dull without the unique energy each friend brings. Whether it's a fresh outlook on the world or a humorous twist on life's big questions, each person adds depth, color, and vibrancy that make every gathering unforgettable.

Ask, Learn & Embrace
How do we use our differences to build stronger bonds? Begin with genuine curiosity. When you find yourself in a situation where someone's viewpoint is unfamiliar or a little out there, lean into it. Instead of dismissing an idea with "That's weird," try saying "Tell me more!" That one simple shift opens the door to understanding

Start by asking your friends about their backgrounds, traditions, and the interests that make them tick (looking at you, vintage-spoon collectors). Be open to their stories, those moments of joy, challenges, and family tales passed down through generations. The more you learn, the richer your friendships become. You may find yourself exploring topics you'd never imagined, from ancient cooking methods to the history behind a cultural tradition.

One day you're swapping travel experiences, and the next, you're booking a trip together to a destination that's meaningful to them, experiencing it through their eyes. Or perhaps, by understanding their approach to life's big questions, you discover new perspectives that shape your own. Embracing each other's differences transforms friendships into journeys of growth and shared discovery, making every conversation an opportunity to broaden your world.

Exploring the Stories Behind the Smiles

It's easy to assume we have nothing in common with someone who sees the world differently, but when you dig deeper, you often uncover surprising connections. Maybe your friend's love for cooking comes from their grandmother's family recipes, cherished memories passed down through generations. You might bond over a similar tradition in your own family, realizing how food ties us to our roots and loved ones. Or there's your friend who's passionate about social justice. They open your eyes to issues you hadn't fully considered, and those late-night talks push you both to explore new perspectives and ways to make a difference.

Then there's the friend who drags you to every indie film premiere. At first, you're skeptical of the quirky plots, but over time, these films spark conversations about storytelling, art, and culture, connecting you in ways that go beyond entertainment. Or perhaps it's your workout buddy who inspires you to train for a marathon together. Crossing that finish line side by side, despite every sore muscle, reminds you of the strength that comes from shared challenges and mutual support.

Each of these experiences reveals what makes each person irreplaceable, offering you a lens into their world, whether it's the values they hold close, the struggles they've faced, or the dreams they're pursuing.

Opposites Laugh Alike

Let's savor the laughs that come with embracing one-of-a-kind personalities and ways of seeing the world. Like that time you went camping with your city-friend who had never set up a tent and somehow packed a portable espresso machine. You both laughed at the contrast in your approaches, creating inside jokes about glamping that still make you laugh years later.

Or dig a little deeper, consider your friend who grew up in a culture where community and family are at the core of everything, while you were raised to value independence and self-reliance. Through conversations, you start to see life through their collective lens, sparking laughs over your different approaches—like their insistence on feeding an entire group while you're still figuring out portions for one. These chats might then lead to unexpected debates on global issues like sustainability or cultural preservation, where you both bring different insights to the table.

It's in these deeper exchanges, with a mix of humor and heart, that you realize diversity of thought isn't just valuable—it's essential. Another worldview enriches your friendship, rooting it in shared values while also opening your mind to ideas you might have overlooked.

A Hot Discovery Beyond the Yoga Studio

Years ago, when a new hot yoga studio opened in town, I was beyond excited. I'd always been interested in yoga but hadn't quite found the right class. This felt like the perfect opportunity to dive in, knowing it would be filled with other beginners ready to try something new. I found a deep sense of peace in that heated room, moving through poses, drenched in sweat, and loving every second of it.

Naturally, I had to share this newfound love with my friends. One friend immediately dismissed the idea—she jokingly called it "barf-oga," convinced the heat would be too much (sometimes it can be). Another friend, though, was curious and agreed to give it a try. She was a morning person and convinced me to join her at a 6am class. That morning, we quietly slipped into the studio, and by the time we were in shavasana, she was hooked. Hot yoga quickly became a shared ritual that added a new dimension to our friendship. Even after she moved away, she kept up the practice, finding a new studio and continuing her yoga journey.

This shared experience strengthened our bond and taught me how rewarding it is to share something you love with your friends. Sometimes, they surprise you and fall in love with it too.

Beyond Small Talk: Diving into the Big Stuff

Then there were my long, thought-provoking conversations with a friend who was deeply engaged in political issues. She brought insights that challenged me to think differently and pushed me to examine my own values on everything from public policy impacts to voting rights. As we discussed topics that felt both personal and far-reaching, I found myself considering perspectives I hadn't fully explored before, whether we agreed or not.

These conversations strengthened our friendship and reminded me of the value in welcoming different viewpoints, as it really does broaden our understanding of the world. Much like practicing yoga together, sharing experiences adds a sense of depth and mutual appreciation to your connection that encourages growth by seeing the world in new ways.

Get Curious: Celebrate the Unique & Unusual!

- **Be Curious About Their World:** Next time a friend shares a unique perspective—whether it's on a big issue or a quirky hobby like extreme ironing (yes, it's real!)—ask questions. Try, "What got you into that?" or "How did you come to think that way?" Diving into their backstory or point of view opens doors to meaningful conversations that can expand your own outlook, even if you don't end up joining in.

- **Embrace a "Yes" Moment:** Challenge yourself to try something new, whether it's sampling a friend's favorite spicy dish, attending an improv night, or discussing their take on a complex topic. Stepping into their world shows a willingness to see things through their eyes, even if it's just for a moment, and may surprise you with what you take away.

- **Experience & Perspective Swap:** Take turns sharing both activities and viewpoints. One week, explore a friend's hiking trail; the next, ask them to share their thoughts on a global issue they care about. These swaps create shared memories and help everyone understand the world a little differently by experiencing it through each other's eyes.

- **Show & Tell for Grown-Ups:** Host a 'Passion and Perspective Party' where friends share their unique interests (eccentric fashion style or offbeat hobby) and their views on topics that fuel their drive, whether it's environmental action or a local cause. Embrace the diversity within your group and celebrate the ideas and quirks that make everyone irreplaceable.

- **Curiosity Chats:** Keep conversations fresh with open-ended questions that go beyond small talk, like "What's a perspective you've recently changed your mind about?" or "What's one thing you've always wanted to try but haven't yet?" This approach makes room for deeper exchanges and helps celebrate the richness of perspectives among our friends. When someone shares an unfamiliar view, respond with "That's interesting—tell me more!" to keep the dialogue open.

- **New Viewpoint Challenge:** Each month, set a goal to engage with a friend's outlook, whether it's through a book they recommend, a topic they're passionate about, or an article they found insightful. It's a small way to embrace their unique views and open yourself up to fresh ideas.

Every eccentric hobby, unexpected opinion, and deep conversation transforms your hangouts into unforgettable adventures. So dive in! Embrace the friend who collects vintage spoons, debate fiercely with the one championing public policy, and take that sunrise yoga class you swore was not your thing. Together, you're crafting memories, sparking laughs, and creating those *Did we really just do that?* moments. Because the best friendships are a dynamic fusion of personalities that make life endlessly fascinating.

40
FROM RIVALS TO ROCK SOLID
Embracing Healthy Competition in Friendships

Who doesn't love a little friendly competition? Whether it's a battle of wits at trivia night, seeing who can run that 5K faster, or even outdoing each other's outfits for a big event, a bit of rivalry can bring much-needed energy into your friendships. But please remember—it's got to stay *friendly*, or things can get dicey. Embrace competition as a way to motivate each other, not as a stealth mission to one-up your bestie. After all, who wants to be that friend who treats every game of Jenga like a demolition derby?

Motivation Mates
With healthy competition in friendships, you get a personal coach, cheerleader, and (occasional) smack-talker all in one package. Maybe you've both set fitness goals, and a little race to the finish line is just the motivation you need to avoid that 7th snooze button in the morning. Or perhaps your friend just learned to bake the world's fluffiest cupcakes, and now you are determined to master that frosting swirl. It's not about who wins or loses—it's about pushing each other to be more awesome than ever. When your friend wins, you *both* win. That's just science!

Friendly Fire, Full of Laughter
There's nothing like a playful rivalry to kick up the joy. From friendly debates over who makes the best espresso martini to an intense game of charades that may or may not get out of hand, these moments should be filled with laughter. Keep things light by poking fun at each other—in a loving way, of course—and keeping the mood fun. If one of you takes a loss seriously, it can turn from fun into something that feels more like a high-stakes poker game. Always remember to laugh it off!

Maybe your friend consistently beats you at mini-golf (they swear it's all skill, but you are suspicious), or maybe you have been undefeated in Uno for the last six game nights. Either way, it's about having fun, not holding grudges. Throw a playful "good game" their way and keep the banter rolling. Extra points if you throw in a "You got lucky this time, but I'll be back!"

Celebrate Wins—Even When They're Not Yours

Healthy competition doesn't mean you have to win all the time—sometimes it's about cheering *loudly* for your friend's success. If they're hitting a milestone or taking it to the next level about something you both care about, hype them up! Strong friendships survive on mutual support, so say, "You totally rocked that!" or "I'm so proud of you for making it happen!" because their win is also a win for the friendship.

The difference between friendly competition and rivalry is that, instead of feeling like their victory is your loss, you are there to celebrate their achievements like they are your own. Besides, you will have your moment to shine soon enough—everyone gets their turn.

Take Five When Tensions Rise

While competition can be fun, it's important to recognize when things are getting too intense. If you or your friend start feeling stressed, frustrated, or like it's becoming less about fun and more about winning, it's time to take a breather. Remember, the goal is to bring out the best in each other, not to create tension or resentment.

It's about balance. So, if things get too competitive, take a break, grab that ice cream and remind each other that the friendship matters more than who wins at trivia night. Besides, it's always more fun when everyone is laughing, not plotting their revenge during the next round of Yahtzee.

A Competitive Boost in the Workout Zone

Andrea and I decided we needed a little extra motivation to stay on track with our fitness goals, so we turned it into a friendly competition. We started off with a pact to meet for morning hikes, gym sessions, and the occasional yoga class, but things quickly escalated when we discovered we could track our progress through the fitness rings on our iPhones. Suddenly, it wasn't just about showing up—it was about who could close their rings faster, and more often.

The first week, we were knocking it out of the park. Every morning, I'd see those little congratulatory messages pop up: 'Andrea closed all her rings!' And you better believe I wasn't about to let her have all the glory. We hiked like we were trying to outpace the sunrise, pushing each other to walk just a little faster, take the steeper trail, or add that extra rep in the gym. We even started texting each other screenshots of our activity rings at the end of the day, with cheeky comments like, "Almost beat you today!" or "I see you slacking—time to step it up tomorrow!"

But then, life happened. Work got hectic, and my motivation hit rock bottom. I had every excuse in the book to skip a workout. Andrea, however, wasn't about to let me off easy. She sent me a text that said, "Hey, I'm planning to close all my rings by noon tomorrow—are we still hitting that gym class, or should I count this as a win?" It was the competitive nudge I needed.

The next morning, I showed up to the gym, determined to close my rings and not let Andrea outpace me. We both knew the competition wasn't about beating each other it was about keeping each other accountable and making sure neither of us lost sight of our goals. Whether it was seeing who could hold a plank the longest or nail a handstand, it turned into this amazing bond where we weren't just workout partners—we were rivals in the best way possible.

And when one of us didn't make it, the other was there with coffee in hand and a, "Don't worry, we'll smash it tomorrow!" That kind of healthy competition, driven by those little fitness rings on our phones, became more than just a challenge—it was our way of showing up for each other, pushing each other to be our best, and keeping our friendship stronger than ever.

Fun & Games: Friendship Edition!

- **Challenge Accepted:** Challenge your friend to a fun goal—whether it's learning a new recipe or tackling a DIY project. Frame it as a fun way to help each other grow: "How about we both try baking sourdough bread this weekend and see who makes the best loaf?" FYI: It's definitely not going to be you on the first try.

- **Win–Win Rewards:** Agree on a reward that benefits both of you, regardless of who 'wins.' For example, "Whoever finishes this book first gets to pick our next hangout spot—and yes, it can involve ice cream." (Ya, I got ice cream on the mind right now...)

- **Turn Losses into Laughs:** Instead of getting hung up on who 'won,' make it a fun tradition. Try saying, "Last place gets to serenade the winner with their go-to karaoke song!" It's impossible to stay frustrated when there's a mini concert involved. Then, take a moment to reflect, asking, "So, what did we take away from that?"

(Besides that maybe you should brush up on your chess skills).

- **Show the Love:** After your friend nails it, take the time to share your excitement for their success. Send a fun voice note or show up with a cupcake that says, "You're awesome!" in frosting.

- **Victory Rituals:** Every time one of you hits a goal, establish a fun ritual, whether it's a Victory Happy Hour or a post-competition debrief where you both relive the highs and laugh at the setbacks.

- **Check the Vibes:** After a competitive moment, ask your friend, "How are you feeling about that? Still fun?" It's a quick way to ensure things stay friendly and light.

- **Recharge Time:** If competition is becoming stressful, suggest a break by saying, "Let's just enjoy a chill day today and save the rivalry for next time."

At the heart of it, healthy competition in friendships is about supporting each other's growth while keeping things fun and light-hearted. You're saying, "I believe in you so much, I know you can do this—and I'll be right there, giving you a run for your money!" Just remember, it's not about winning—think about how you both grow, challenge, and uplift each other along the way.

So, throw down that friendly challenge, have a blast, and keep the love flowing—even if you *totally* destroy them at Scrabble next time. Let the games begin!

CONCLUSION
Embrace Your Tribe, Embrace Yourself

Our friendships reflect who we are, where we've been, and where we're headed. The people we choose to surround ourselves with are more than just companions—they're partners in our growth, mirrors of our values, and supporters through all the ups and downs. Together, we form *Fun, Fierce, and Forever Friendships* that embrace every unique aspect of who we are. Even though this book might feel like a LOT, the intent is simple—to bring a bit more awareness to your day-to-day connections. If you walk away with just one or two ideas that resonate, that's a success.

This journey of finding, nurturing, and appreciating your tribe is just as much about discovering who you are. The more you understand your own needs, values, and boundaries, the more you'll attract friendships that genuinely enrich your life. At the heart of it all, remember—the most important relationship is the one you have with yourself. When that foundation is strong, every other connection thrives. And while not every friend will belong in your inner circle, each connection has its own special value, whether they're your shoulder to lean on, your spontaneous adventure buddy, or your thoughtful confidante.

Our friendships come from all walks of life, shaped by different cultures, backgrounds, and experiences. And when we see each other as extraordinary individuals, beyond labels and differences, we open ourselves up to learning so much more. Your friendships are evolving as much as you are, and they're shaped by time, experience, and love. Don't be afraid to grow, let go, or reach out when life calls for change.

Whether you're planting new seeds or nurturing roots that have been there for years, be intentional in how you show up for your friends and for yourself. Friendship is a garden that thrives on care, connection, and a whole lot of love. Keep tending to it, and watch it blossom into something truly remarkable. Trust me, this garden is going to be a masterpiece.

ACKNOWLEDGMENTS

To my life partner, Benito, who believed in me from the moment the thought of this book was born and never let me doubt myself for a second. Thank you for being my unwavering rock through it all.

To my Auntie Karen, for sending me hundreds of quotes that kept my inspiration alive. You braved my first rough draft, providing feedback and sparking ideas along the way.

To Jenn, who walked back into my life at just the right time with her charisma, charm, and boundless encouragement. You brought sunshine into every day and helped make the writing process a little easier with your smiles and bestie vibes.

To Kim, my friend from my old hometown, for all those late-night calls and your random check ins to say, "Hey, I've got this story—maybe it'll work for that chapter!" Thank you for being that true inner-circle friend who kept me top of mind.

To Anna, my old neighbor, confidant and superhero. You kept me on deadlines, gave the most honest feedback, and shared your stories to help bring so much life to these pages.

To my kids—Keilen, Logan, and Gabi—and the other young people in my life whom I love as my own, thank you for keeping me grounded, always bringing humor and joy, and reminding me what truly matters.

To my inner circle crew—Aisha, Wendy, Heather, Kacy, Jodi, Jodi, Jody (yes, that many!), Amy, Martina and Hallie. Thank you for listening to my crazy ideas, standing by my side, and sharing in the memories that have filled my life with meaning.

To Petra, my morning walking buddy and neighbor, who has spent countless hours helping me brainstorm at 6am during our three-mile walks. Thank you for being there to listen to all my yammering about this chapter or the real-life inspirations behind it.

To Coach Patti, who helped me grow, mature, and evolve through this journey.

To my new gal pal Alisha, who stepped into my life this year—a year of big changes—and was there to help me 'get through' on some of the tougher days. Thank you for being that unexpected, steady support when I needed it most.

To Sandra, my talented designer, who gave me the simple, powerful advice to "just write for 20 minutes." That 20 minutes turned into 60, and eventually, 12–hour days, as the words started to flow.

To Jean and Tameiko, my work buddies for life!

And finally, to my parents—thank you for raising such an awesome daughter!

This book wouldn't have happened without you all.
Thank you for being my tribe.

NOTE: *The names used to tell the stories have been changed to respect the privacy of my friends, but rest assured, the vibes are 100% authentic and the stories are a path to something beautiful. Welcome to my tribe and enjoy the journey!*

APPENDIX
Quick Guide to Friendship Topics

Communication
Chapters 5, 7, 8, 9, 10, 14, 21, 32
Communication is the heartbeat of any meaningful friendship. These chapters delve into the art of giving timely feedback, addressing sensitive topics, and supporting friends through challenges with empathy and clarity. Discover tools to ensure your friends feel heard and valued, whether through lighthearted chats or deep conversations. From offering heartfelt apologies to balancing self-reflection with connection, you'll find practical advice for building trust, fostering understanding, and strengthening bonds that last.

Disagreements & Conflict Resolution
Chapters 11, 14, 22, 23, 24, 25, 26, 28
Every friendship faces challenges, but conflicts don't have to spell trouble. These chapters explore how to navigate disagreements with empathy, set boundaries with care, and turn tension into opportunities for growth. From addressing jealousy and misunderstandings to learning when to press pause or let go, you will find applicable strategies for maintaining respect and keeping your bonds strong, even in tough times.

Workplace Friends
Chapter 36
Balancing friendships in the workplace requires a unique approach. This chapter explores maintaining professional boundaries while fostering meaningful connections, managing office politics with integrity, and building mutual support to thrive together in any work setting.

Married Friends & Navigating Life Changes
Chapters 29, 31, 33
Life changes impact friendships, especially as friends get married, have children, or go through major personal transitions. Here, you'll learn to adapt and support your friends as they navigate new roles and responsibilities, finding ways to stay connected and evolve alongside one another.

Emotional Support
Chapters 21, 27, 37
Friends are often the lifeline through life's toughest and most joyful moments. Here, you'll uncover ways to offer unwavering support without judgment, create a safe haven for open sharing, and show up with compassion and commitment when it matters most. Whether it's navigating challenges together or being their go-to person in a crisis, discover the art of being a dependable, understanding friend.

Personal Growth and Authenticity
Chapters 3, 4, 12, 13
Personal growth flourishes in authentic friendships. These chapters encourage you to be genuine with your friends, embrace vulnerability, and support each other's individual journeys. You'll find tips on creating a growth-oriented atmosphere where everyone can thrive as their true selves.

Celebration and Supporting Success
Chapters 19, 39
Celebrate each other's achievements with joy! In these chapters, discover ways to uplift and cheer on friends' successes without jealousy or competition, and find meaningful ways to acknowledge wins of all sizes, creating a positive and supportive environment.

Diversity and Collective Friendship
Chapters 16, 38, 39
Friendships are richer with diversity and inclusion. These chapters explore how to honor differences, celebrate varied perspectives, and build connections that go beyond surface-level similarities, creating a collective of supportive and unique individuals.

Care and Loyalty
Chapters 1, 2, 6, 15, 22, 34, 35, 37
Trust and loyalty serve as the backbone of enduring friendships. Here you will uncover the importance of consistent actions—offering support, expressing gratitude, and creating balance—to nurture meaningful connections. Explore how focused attention, thoughtful gestures, and a commitment to growth can strengthen relationships, from addressing distractions to reconnecting after distance or navigating shared spaces. By prioritizing small but intentional efforts, friendships can thrive and stand the test of time.

Friendship Fun and Playful Connections
Chapters 17, 18, 20, 30, 40
Injecting fun and friendly competition can energize and deepen friendships. Here we explore how shared interests, lighthearted challenges, and playful activities create memorable connections. Whether it's collaborating on tech-inspired adventures, sharing playlists, planning exciting outings, or fostering healthy competition, these ideas make friendships dynamic and rewarding. Dive into ways to balance camaraderie and fun, ensuring every moment strengthens your bond and brings plenty of laughter.

www.ingramcontent.com/pod-product-compliance
Lightning Source LLC
Chambersburg PA
CBHW051541020426
42333CB00016B/2032